# My Emmaus

*God is Faithful 24/7*

## Mike Parker

*Be blessed as you read!*
*In Christ,*
*Mike Parker*
*Eph. 3:20-21*

*cell: 229-815-6814*

Copyright © 2017 **Mike Parker**

All rights reserved. No part of this publication may be reproduced or transmitted in any form or by any electronic or mechanical means including photo copying, recording, or any information storage and retrieval system now known or to be invented, without permission in writing from the publisher or the author.

ISBN-13: 978-1-945975-45-5

All Scripture quotations, unless otherwise indicated, are from The ESV Bible (The Holy Bible, English Standard Version) copyright © 2001 by Crossway Bibles, a publishing ministry of Good News Publishers. Unauthorized reproduction of this publication is prohibited. All rights reserved.

Scripture quotations marked KJV, are from The King James Version. The KJV is public domain in the United States.

Published by EA Books Publishing, a division of
Living Parables of Central Florida, Inc. a 501c3

EABooksPublishing.com

# Dedication

This book is dedicated to the people who have been presented through the pages of 'My Emmaus'. Without them this collection of inspirational short stories would not have been possible.

A special dedication is reserved for my loving wife, Jan, and our two sons, Jake and Ben

# Content

| | |
|---|---|
| Dedication | iii |
| Contents | iv |
| Preface | v |
| Chapter One – On the Road to Emmaus | 1 |
| Chapter Two – Fasting for Children | 6 |
| Chapter Three – Here Comes Fred | 13 |
| Chapter Four – One Whale of a Storm | 27 |
| Chapter Five - You Can't Out-Give God! | 34 |
| Chapter Six – Distractions | 42 |
| Chapter Seven - Here Comes the Bride | 49 |
| Chapter Eight - Freedom from Fear and the Warrior's Armor | 57 |
| Chapter Nine - Fasting for Children – Part Two | 67 |
| Chapter Ten - God Is Faithful 24/7 | 73 |
| Chapter Eleven - A Wolf in Sheepdog's Clothing | 84 |
| Chapter Twelve - A Bad Case of Déjà vu | 89 |
| Chapter Thirteen - A Mama With "Angry Birds" in Her Head | 95 |
| Chapter Fourteen - She Likes Me She Likes Me Not | 99 |
| Chapter Fifteen – Shaq Time | 102 |
| Chapter Sixteen - Red-Headed Bama Fan | 109 |
| Epilogue | 117 |
| A Prayer for Salvation | 119 |
| A Prayer from Ephesians 1:17-20 | 120 |
| A Prayer from Ephesians 3:16-20 | 120 |

# Preface

King David reminds us in Psalm 23:3 that the Lord our Shepherd, restores our souls and leads us in paths of righteousness for His names sake. You will find as you peruse the pages of 'My Emmaus' that this restoration and encouragement of our souls is a continual process. It begins with the grace and mercy of a loving savior chasing us down with the provision found on His cross and in His resurrection. Then it continues throughout a life-time of obedience and missteps as He provides the water that quenches our thirst.

Jesus is the original 'Son of Encouragement'. The disciples on the road to Emmaus came to that realization when their eyes were opened to His abiding presence. As you read this manuscript may the water of God, Christ the living word, wash over you removing all hindrances of sight, and create within you a greater hunger for more of Himself. I hope that you enjoy your journey through these practical pages and that in doing so you find divine restoration in the presence of God.

*Chapter One*

# *On the Road to Emmaus*

*They said to each other, "Did not our hearts burn within us while he talked to us on the road, while he opened to us the Scriptures?"* **Luke 24:32**

We all have our favorite scriptures. Many offer encouragement and strength; still others offer hope and love. No matter the takeaway, they always seem to inspire us at just the right time. One of my favorite scriptures is Luke 24:13-35. In this passage, we see two friends, discouraged by recent events, walking along a dry and dusty road toward the small town of Emmaus.

Their discouragement was intense, especially after the tortuous flogging and crucifixion of their savior and His death and burial. Just that morning, some of the women in their group had reported that He had risen from the dead. Oh, how they wanted to believe, but doubt and despair settled over them like a dark cloud.

*My Emmaus*

Yes, their grief, still so fresh, had all but banished any sense of hope. Overwhelming discouragement was robbing the very life from their souls. Yet deep down, shrouded in those layers of discouragement, was a glimmer of light, a smoldering wick of hope that just needed the Messiah's very breath to cause it to flicker and come a blaze.

But back in their present reality, we see the two tired, confused and broken friends recollecting the what-ifs and if-onlys of their experience. Obviously, the pair was greatly startled when a stranger appeared beside them. They failed to realize that this stranger did not merely overtake them on the road but rather materialized out of nothing.

Each time I read this part of the story, I always chuckle at our Savior's sense of humor. As if Captain Kirk beaming down from the Starship Enterprise, Jesus arrived—but with holy camouflage disguising His identity. In that moment, Star Trek met Mission Possible. Unrecognized, Jesus asked them about their conversation, and Cleopas (whom I will call Cleo) replies, "Are you the only clueless person within miles of Jerusalem regarding the things concerning Jesus?" (That was a paraphrase.)

With his sense of humor intact, Jesus replies, "What things?"

While we are chuckling, let me interject here that we do not know the name of the other disciple. With a friend named Cleo, though, we can easily imagine that His friend could have been

Bubba. Cleo and Bubba, a couple of good old boys from southern Israel.

Cleo is astonished at the stranger's lack of knowledge, so he explains everything in great detail. The Jewish leaders turning Jesus over to the Romans for crucifixion. The women finding the tomb empty and the declaration of the angels.

To this Jesus replies, "O foolish ones, and slow of heart to believe all that the prophets have spoken! Was it not necessary that the Christ should suffer these things and enter into His glory?" Then, beginning with Moses and all the Prophets, He interpreted to them in all the Scriptures the things concerning himself (Luke 24:25-27).

The miles began to click off with rapidity as Cleo and Bubba listened intently to the stranger's teaching. Not only that, but the dimmed smoldering in their souls began to flicker as the unrecognized Savior breathed into them the words of life.

As they neared town, Jesus acted as though He would continue farther, but Cleo and Bubba asked Him to stay with them and be refreshed. Jesus agreed and took the initiative in the pre-meal ritual of blessing and breaking the bread. Suddenly, Jesus' travel companions had their eyes opened and they realized that the stranger was in fact Jesus Himself, the Lamb of God.

Another Star Trek moment came, and Jesus vanished from their midst. This left Cleo and Bubba in a state of amazement and absolute belief in the resurrection. They quite literally had living proof. No quibbling about it, this was indeed the Savior, Christ the Lord, risen from the grave.

What a game changer! Now their souls became a raging fire. With this intense burning, Cleo and Bubba asked one another, "Did not our hearts burn within us while He talked to us on the road, while He opened to us the Scriptures?" (Luke 24:32)

With new life, energy and a sense of urgency they immediately hurried to Jerusalem. Can you picture them half running and walking and then sprinting the last hundred yards to the place of meeting? In their excitement, they fling open the door and dash stumblingly up the stairs to get to the disciples. For a few winded seconds, Cleo and Bubba can only gasp and pant, but their faces radiate a message of sheer joy!

And then it happens. Having just received the greatest encouragement of their lives, the two friends find themselves encouraging the disciples and their guests. Since that night, Cleo and Bubba's story of a wise, loving, and humorous savior has encouraged and inspired millions.

Cleo and Bubba truly had a memorable day. Early that morning they heard the personal accounts of others, experienced Jesus themselves on the road to Emmaus, and then saw Him again firsthand when he appeared to the larger group later that evening. I know some of you are thinking, "Wow, if I could just experience Jesus the way Cleo and Bubba did, then there wouldn't be any room in my life for doubt." You mean you have more in common with Thomas than Cleo and Bubba. Join the club!

Thomas was the only one of the eleven disciples that was not in the room that evening. In his own words, he needed tangible proof or he wouldn't believe. Thomas eventually got the proof he was looking for, but Jesus rebuked him for his unbelief by saying, "Blessed are those who have not seen and yet believe." (John 20:29)

The truth is that we all have had our own share of Emmaus moments with Jesus: times of peace, financial interventions, healings, encouraging moments with friends and loved ones and others too numerous to number. Sometimes we just need to stop and consider those heart-burning experiences. While reading this book, you should do just that — pause and reflect on the goodness of God.

For now, I hope the rest of this reading lifts your soul and strengthens your resolve to press on with Jesus as I share with you some of my own Emmaus moments. Those were the times when Jesus came along side me on a dry, dusty road and breathed into me the words of life. Walk with me, will you, and be encouraged — or if need be, let the Holy Spirit fan the smoldering embers of your own soul into a fresh, glowing flame.

*Chapter Two*

# *Fasting for Children*

*"This kind can come forth by nothing, but prayer and fasting."* **Mark 9:29 (KJV)**

In August of 1992, I moved from helping nine special-needs students in a self-contained classroom to literally helping everyone as an assistant principal at Irwin County High School. It was my first administrative position, and I was beyond excited about the new opportunity.

Usually you interview with the principal and then meet with the superintendent for final approval. However, the principal would not be available for another week. So we got ahead a little bit, and I interviewed with the superintendent and his assistant.

The interview was going great, and just one last question remained. Mr. Gentry, the superintendent, smiled. "Mike, tell us why you're the best person for this job."

I took a deep breath and answered in a way that I had not anticipated.

Traditionally, the response to such a question would result in a lengthy synopsis of all my positive qualities—but not this time. An alternative reply had instantly formulated in my mind and spirit, ready to spill out of my mouth. It could cost me the position if these gentlemen were not strong men of faith. But the answer was like fire in my bones and I was all in, so I took a chance.

"Gentlemen, I first have to say that there isn't anything of myself that is remotely good. The only good things in me are my Lord and Savior Jesus Christ and the gifts and talents that He has deposited within me. I do believe, though, that He has called me to be an administrator and that this is the right opportunity."

I will never forget what happened next. Mr. Gentry's smile widened, and he leaned forward. "Son, we don't have a problem with that. You are speaking our language." He then ended the interview by saying that he would have principal Bobby Griffin call me for a follow-up interview when he got home.

A week later, Mr. Griffin met me at school and interviewed me for about ten minutes. Finally he said, "Come with me, Mike. I need to go buy a pecan shaker." That was the beginning of a friendship and mentor/mentee relationship that continues to this day.

About now some of you may be asking what does all this have to do with fasting for children? Well, I am glad you asked. One of my new responsibilities as assistant principal was to serve as the liaison between the school and the system's pregnant student education program. For safety and emotional reasons, pregnant students got the opportunity to attend a self-contained, off-campus program where they learned not only their academic lessons but also how to care for an infant child. Also, the program provided a positive learning environment that allowed each girl to continue her studies while taking care of her baby for the first six weeks following delivery.

That first year, we had about ten girls take part in the parenting program. In the meantime, my wife and I were trying to start a family of our own. Nearly two years passed, and we hadn't had any success; but the teenage girls didn't slow their fertility rate. Girls kept rotating in and out of the program, and one day a renegade thought invaded my mind: "Look at these girls sinning and getting pregnant so easily. You and your wife have done everything right — married as virgins, served God — and you can't even get pregnant. What is fair about that?"

In my mind, I was quick to agree. So much for spiritual warfare. At that point, my own self-righteousness became far more odious than the poor self-control of some of the teenagers I served.

Jan and I finally decided we would help God out a little bit by taking a fertility drug. After a month of that, we both feared that instead of one screaming baby, we could have a whole flock of them. Down the drain went the fertility drug, but the aching in our hearts remained.

One day, a new thought bombarded my mind and spirit—fasting and praying for us to be able to conceive. I read all the scriptures I could related to fasting. Ultimately one verse stood out: Mark 9:29. Jesus' disciples had been trying to cast out a demon from a young boy, and Jesus was nowhere around. When Jesus did return, He rebuked His disciples for their lack of faith and then turned to the demon and cast him out of the boy. The demon didn't go quietly, but he went nonetheless. After all, he was dealing with the creator of the universe.

Jesus' words set that young boy free, and He will do the same for you and me. What power we have in our corner! The amazed disciples asked why they couldn't cast out the demon themselves. Jesus replied in Mark 9:29 (KJV), "This kind can come forth by nothing but prayer and fasting."

That was our answer. We had prayed to have children to no avail, but prayer and fasting would be our winning combination.

The next week, I fasted and prayed for three days that we would conceive a child. After my fast, Jan and I continued enjoying life together and looked expectantly to the future.

Seven weeks later, Jan said that something wasn't right and asked me to take her to the hospital. Throughout the fifteen-minute drive she never complained, even though I knew she was in great pain.

At the emergency room, the doctor made some quick observations and ordered some tests. He quickly returned. "I have some good news and some bad news. The good news is that you are pregnant, and the bad news is that you are pregnant in your fallopian tube."

We needed to operate as soon as possible because Jan was at seven weeks, and the tube threatened to burst. From one test, the doctor could pinpoint the date of conception — the exact date that I ended my fast.

The operation and Jan's recovery went great and the doctor managed to save her fallopian tube. We had much to be thankful for. As I drove home by myself, I plugged in a praise tape and immediately cried with joy. My wife was going to be just fine, and God had healed us so we could conceive.

A few months later, I started getting up early in the morning and having a real quiet time with God. During that time of prayer and worship, I would read one of the Psalms. One morning in early August, the week of planning for teachers, I felt led to read Psalm 43. My Bible fell open to Isaiah 43. I thought it was just a coincidence but decided to read it anyway. I read almost the entire chapter, and then these words jumped off the page at me: "Put Me in remembrance, let us argue together; set forth your case, that you may be proved right." (Isaiah 43:26)

Immediately, children came to mind. Shaken, humbled, awed, and even afraid, I got on my knees. "Father, forgive me if I come too boldly before You, but I believe I would be disobedient to not address You with my case. I am the husband of one wife, and You have allowed me to preach from time to time, but I don't have any children to keep in subjection. Isn't it time, Father, for us to have children?"

I went on with my quiet time, interceded for others, and then just got quiet before the Lord. I was not used to doing that. Soon a thought started coming clear that we would have one or two children on the way by Christmas. Strangely, my mind wouldn't settle on one or two, but I wrote it in my journal and then really got excited. We were going to be parents!

When I got to school, I went straight to our French teacher, Martha Coley, a dear friend and prayer partner, and told her about my experience. She believed that God would accomplish exactly what He had promised.

Later that morning, Mr. Griffin sent me to the convenience store to pick up some drinks for our department head meeting. After I paid, the cashier started counting my change and then stopped. "You don't want this dollar bill."

I told her, "Yes I do."

"No, you don't; let me read it to you." She read the message someone had written on the margin of the bill out loud for me and the other four customers in line, "You are going to have two kids."

I laughed and then told her and the customers all about my morning. They were all stunned, and I walked out with a dollar bill that Jan and I would laminate and save to this day.

*My Emmaus*

Driving back to school, I kept glancing at the squiggly handwriting on the bill. I envisioned a little old lady in her own quiet time obediently responding to the Holy Spirit's prompting to scribble that faith-affirming and confirming message on its margin. All of this happened on a Friday morning, and the next evening we conceived a child.

That pregnancy would go full term, and the resulting baby boy, Jake, is now in graduate school. Two years and three months after Jake's birth, we had another boy, Ben, who is a sophomore in college. Two incredible young men. God is faithful!

Do you have your own challenges from time to time that seem larger than life, so that you don't know where to begin? May I suggest that you consider a little fasting to go along with your praying? Remember, Jesus rebuked his disciples not for their lack of effort but of faith. Fasting is essentially a humbling of oneself before God and serves to build us up in our most holy faith. It really can make a difference.

So, bon appétit!

I mean, happy fasting.

*Chapter Three*

# *Here Comes Fred*

*"Go therefore and make disciples of all nations, baptizing them in the name of the Father of the Son and of the Holy Spirit."* **Matthew 28:19**

July loomed hot and wet for sure. We were still on schedule to move into the new Irwin County High School campus, but all the rain had delayed a myriad of things, like asphalt for entrances and parking lots. We had just gotten the news that we were going to open the new school in August as planned, but substituting for that asphalt would be natural Georgia red clay!

With so much rain, we would never keep all that clay out of the school. Life can be like that sometimes. Just when you think you have it all figured out, things can get a little messy. A brand-new school with red clay ground into all its carpeting would be about as beautiful as a cheerleader squad caught in a thunderstorm with too much mascara. Yikes!

That afternoon, I gave a school tour to a group of foreign exchange student consultants. I had a great time showing off all the innovative features of our trend-setting facility. The idea of hosting a foreign exchange student seized my interest.

At home, I talked to Jan about the possibility. Her initial and final response was that we shouldn't until we had teenagers of our own. I am blessed to have married a wise and discerning lady, so I completely concurred with her evaluation and banished the idea from my mind.

Now, let's skip forward to that day when I got the dollar bill. As if that day wasn't already earth shaking and faith building enough, another opportunity just as powerful beckoned.

I had basked all morning in my unequivocal belief that Jan would be pregnant any day. After we all got back from lunch, I noticed Robert Winter in the front office installing our school's alarm system. I walked toward him to see how it was going.

Before I got there, he snatched up a manila folder and handed it to me with a smile. "Mike, the Lord told me to give this to you."

"What is it?"

"It is information about Fred, a foreign exchange student, and the Lord clearly told me he was to be in your home."

I didn't even know that Robert dealt with foreign exchange students. In fact, he'd had dozens in his home over the years. Some even stayed in America and went to work for him.

I asked, "If we take Fred, when would we need to pick him up?"

"Tomorrow, that is when everyone else will be getting theirs." Robert never broke his confident and reassuring smile.

Obviously, my next question was, "Why so quick?"

"He was supposed to go to a family in Alabama, but something has come up, and now they are not able to take him."

"Well, can I let you know this evening? I need to sit down and talk to my wife about the opportunity." I knew that Jan and I had already made an educated decision not to have any foreign exchange students in the next decade or two.

"Sure thing." Robert walked back toward the alarm panel.

I took the package home and laid it on the table. I would be working late that afternoon, so Jan would beat me home by about an hour. Therefore, I called her office and left a message for her to look at the package on the table and that we would talk about it when I got home.

The rest of that afternoon passed uneventfully. Sometime around 6:30 p.m. I headed home. I made it up the steps but never got a word in!

Jan met me at the door, tears in her eyes. "We have to take him. The Holy Spirit is very clear about this. We have to take him."

Did I not tell you I had a special wife? Every man needs one as wise, discerning, and diligent as she. And diligent is the appropriate word. She immediately went into preparation mode.

*My Emmaus*

Before we settled in for the night, Fred had a room fit for a teenage boy, and we had the fridge and the cupboards stocked and ready for his arrival. Can you say Proverbs 31 woman? Absolutely!

The next morning, a representative from the exchange student program brought Fred to our door. All he had for luggage was a bag with a few belongings. Jan and I realized that Fred would need a complete wardrobe, so we made a quick Wal-Mart run. By the end of the day, it was as if Fred had always been with us. He quickly became a joy to have around.

At age sixteen, Fred had already survived a civil war in his country, and it had taken a great toll on food and necessities. During that time, meat was a real luxury. Worse yet, his family had eleven mouths to feed — seven of them sharing one bedroom.

With that in mind, let me share an interesting scenario from our first weekend together. Right away Fred realized that our neighborhood had dozens of squirrels, and that most of them were in our backyard. Jan noticed Fred picking up rocks out of the driveway and asked him why.

"Mom, with these rocks I will kill many squirrels, and we will have an abundance of meat. This is good."

Jan mentioned it to me, and I took Fred to our freezer, full of venison, fish, and beef. "See, we already have an abundance of all kinds of meat." For that revelation, Fred was exceedingly grateful, and so were the squirrels.

*God is Faithful 24/7*

Our first week together was one of adjustment. Jan and I had always had the house to ourselves. Suddenly we had a son, one that didn't need diaper changes or tending during the night. And the biggest surprise of all, boy could he eat!

A couple of weeks later, we took Fred to a state park for an induction meeting with all the other foreign exchange students and their host parents. Many of the students in the program had a federal grant paying some of their costs. This funding was for students from former Soviet Union satellite nations. For security reasons, I can't tell you where our son was from.

At the park, the leaders split us up, into host parents and students and spoke to us separately. Afterward, we met up with Fred and headed to the car. We had quite a few miles to travel to get home and plenty of time to talk about the day's events.

Asked if anything exciting happened during their meeting, Fred smiled wide. "Yeah, Dad! They were speaking with us about abstaining from sexual relations while we are in America. All of a sudden, a girl from Brazil jumped up and said that she didn't care what they said. That she came to America to have sex with as many American boys as she could, and that was exactly what she was going to do."

I said, "You can't be serious."

"No, really."

## My Emmaus

"Fred, that just isn't right. Sex should be saved for marriage. You haven't had sex yet, have you?"

"Oh, yes! Hundreds of times. Practice makes perfect."

Jan and I stared at each other, mortified. My career flashed before my eyes.

At this point I need to clarify for you exactly who we had in our back seat. The name Fred probably has you picturing Fred Savage as the all-American Wonder Years boy. Or perhaps a popular brand of chewable vitamin. Forget that image.

Don't picture Fred, picture Aladdin. He was a dashing, tanned, pearly-toothed, dreamy eyed, charming Casanova with thick, dark hair. And I had turned this guy loose on Irwin County High School. I could almost see the execution drummer smiling while Mr. Griffin sadly shared with me the Board of Education was terminating my employment.

For just a moment let me skip ahead about twenty years. Fred came back to see us a few years ago, and I asked him about that day. He didn't remember making those remarks. He simply smiled and said, "Dad, that was just teenage bull sugar," except he didn't say sugar. After all those years, I finally found out that all my fears were groundless. Hallelujah!

Fred was an instant hit at school. Remember, he looked and sounded like Aladdin. This smooth-talking rascal would flirt with a girl and then flash a smile and say, "My heart tells me that you are mine." A great line even by itself, but the accent was the clincher.

Now that you can properly picture Fred, I can add that he was Muslim-a real Aladdin. Nevertheless, he consistently went to church with us. Our congregation met for services in our pastor's home, and I served as the worship leader. I still recall the incredible experience of watching Fred interact with everyone as if he had known them all his life.

About a month after Fred arrived, he awoke one Saturday morning looking sleepless and fearful. "Dad, during the night I awoke and found a large black bear on top of me with burning red eyes and terrible teeth. He felt so heavy on me that I couldn't breathe! He was literally crushing the life out of me. Finally, he vanished.

"I knew instantly that it was Allah sending me a message that I needed to start praying toward Mecca five times a day."

Immediately, I knew that we had a situation. When Fred came to America, he signed an agreement that he would not practice the strict tenets of his faith while a foreign exchange student because it would disrupt the school day. If he violated that agreement, he would have to go back to his country. I knew that the Lord had sent us Fred, and this was a spiritual attack designed to steal Fred from us. Then he could not know the truth and have the truth set him free. I invited Fred to go walk the track with me.

*My Emmaus*

Our house was just a few hundred yards from the track. As we walked around the track Fred related his concerns. He believed he didn't have a choice.

Instead of immediately bringing up the obvious problem, I asked, "Fred, what was the angry-looking bear on your chest?"

"A messenger of Allah!"

"Fred, the vision you experienced, was it a vision of love or a vision of hate?"

"It was a vision of hate."

"Fred, you have been with us long enough to know that Jan and I are Christians, and we serve Christ the Lord. Based on what you have witnessed, is He a God of hate or a God of love?"

"Oh, He is most assuredly a God of love."

"Fred, Jesus said that He has come to give you life and to give it to you abundantly. You need to know that this God of love is also able to protect you from all harm."

"Yes, Sir!"

I then let Fred know that he had a choice to make. One option would allow him to stay, and the other would send him back to his country, but only he could make that decision.

In the following days, Jan and I prayed earnestly for Fred. Ultimately, Fred never mentioned it again nor did he act on it. He had taken a step closer to this God of love that he was hearing so much about.

A couple of weeks later, Fred revealed that this wasn't his only vision. The first vision came the day before he found out he was coming to America. "I was standing outside and looked up into the sky and saw this glorious vision. In the middle of the radiant clouds was a man dressed in a shining white robe. I couldn't see his face because it was turned, but he was riding on a golden elephant and motioning toward himself with his hand. Dad, what did that mean?"

I lowered my head and prayed, asking the Lord for wisdom. I looked up at Fred with a great sense of wonder. "Fred, Jesus allowed you to see a vision of himself wearing a robe of righteousness in brilliant white while riding on a golden elephant. An elephant that you would recognize as being fit for a king. Jesus was motioning for you to follow Him. Fred, you have done that so far by following Him to America, but your journey is not complete. He wants you to follow Him as Lord and Savior."

I also explained that Jesus was turned away because His face is so radiant that no one can look at it.

"Thank you, Dad, wow!"

As the year went by, many people continued to pray for Fred. Throughout the remainder of his stay, we could often hear Fred singing his favorite praise song: "How lovely on the mountains are the feet of him, who brings good news, good news, announcing peace, proclaiming news of happiness, our God reigns, our God reigns!"

He sang it everywhere, in the shower, raking the yard, and while playing tennis for the high school. It always warmed my heart because I knew by faith that Fred would one day share the news of Jesus Christ and His love while traveling the mountains of his country, and his feet would indeed be beautiful.

Fred had a grand time over the next few months and then he got to experience spring break in America at good old Panama City Beach, Florida. He traveled under the supervision of another family with a foreign exchange student.

He returned home with hundreds of pictures of himself holding gorgeous, bikini-clad girls to his side. I could almost hear him saying, "My heart tells me that you are mine!"

After Fred returned from the beach, Jan and I had to decide whether to let him go to a party at a local farm with a bunch of his classmates. We knew some of the people attending, so we let him go. I arranged for Mr. Griffin's son, Stuart, to bring Fred home.

I heard later that Fred had a pretty good time. A good enough time to have to try to sneak into the house. Before Fred got home, I was already asleep, but Mama Jan was not going to slumber until her son from another mother was home safe.

Sometime after midnight, Stuart dropped Fred off. Jan woke me. "I hear Fred trying to come through his bedroom window. Go greet him."

I went to Fred's room and caught him with one leg in and barely holding on to the windowsill. "Fred what are you doing? We do have a front door, you know. Go to the door, and I will let you in."

"Yes, Sir!"

He met me at the door, and I told him that we would talk in the morning.

Sometimes, someone who has done wrong needs some time to think about it. Well, the next morning Fred felt terrible about the previous evening, especially his shame-laced entry method. I saw the perfect opportunity to address the importance of doing the right thing, even after you've made a mistake. In short, I took it as another opportunity for Fred to experience love and forgiveness.

A few weeks later, about a month before Fred was to leave for home, he had another vivid vision. "I was in my country standing waist deep in a great lake. I had a large basket that I used to dip into the water, and when I would bring the basket up, it had many large fish in it. I kept doing this over and over. What does it mean, Dad?"

*My Emmaus*

Stunned, I immediately knew how to answer him. "Fred, the lake represents your country, and the fish represent the people of your country. God is going to use you as a fisher of people when you return to your native land. Many will come to faith in Jesus as their Lord and Savior. The shallowness of the water is to let you know that it will be easy fishing. The Holy Spirit will do the work. You only have to be obedient to witness of God's great love. You will be living your favorite song. Your feet will be beautiful, the one who brings good news."

Fred nodded. "Yes, Sir!"

A few days later, I realized Jan and I were nearing the end of our time as Fred's American parents. That night, Jan woke me about 2 a.m. "Fred's in his room crying." I wasn't fully alert, so she shook me. "Mike, Fred is crying in his bedroom. Go check on him." Now I heard him.

I went to Fred's room and found him sitting cross-legged on his bed, hands in his lap with tears streaming down his face.

"Fred what's wrong?" I hoped with all my heart that the time had actually arrived that Fred would know Jesus as his Savior and Lord.

"Dad, I am so dirty!"

"What do you mean by being dirty?"

"I have a dirty heart that needs to be cleaned."

"Fred, you have learned since you have been with us how much God loves you. Do you understand that Jesus died on the cross to pay the penalty for your dirty heart?"

"Yes, Sir."

I probed further. "Do you understand that He also rose from the grave and is now seated at the right hand of the Father, interceding for you?"

"Yes, Sir."

"Fred, if you call on Jesus to forgive you of your sin and believe that He rose from the dead, you will be saved and get a new, clean heart. You will be what the Bible calls born again to a new life in Christ Jesus. Is that what you want to do?"

"Yes, Sir, with all of my heart."

I led Fred in a simple prayer of salvation. He called on Jesus to forgive him, to be his Lord and Savior, and spoke his belief that Jesus had risen from the dead. Truly beautiful.

I hugged Fred, and then he went and told Jan. We had an emotional moment for sure.

Jan and I went back to bed knowing that we had become part of a truly amazing story. God's love and relentless pursuit of a teenage Muslim boy changed not only his life, but also the lives of countless others, and especially his American host parents.

*My Emmaus*

Everyone in our little church was ecstatic, and word spread fast about Fred's conversion. Two weeks later, I got to baptize Fred in a local swimming pool. Of course, Fred wanted to sing, "how beautiful on the mountains are the feet of him who brings good news."

Two local congregations wanted to hear Fred give his testimony before he left. Fred did an amazing job, and both congregations took up a love offering for him. They were very generous. When Fred boarded his plane, he had ten hundred-dollar bills in the soles of his shoes.

Fred hated to leave us, and likewise we hated to see him go. I will always remember Fred bending over to kiss our two-week-old son, Jake, before leaving. He smiled wide. "See you later, little brother!" Yes, tears did follow.

Over the years, we have kept in touch with Fred, and he is still doing well. Lord willing, I will get to travel to his country one day and minster by his side. Fred has led several people to the Lord there, and the best is yet to come.

How can we get the good news of the gospel to all the world? There are many ways with modern technology, but I can't think of anything more profound and powerful than a foreign exchange student program. Would you consider such an opportunity? In many cases, you can pick your student, or you can let God surprise you. Who knows? You might even get an upgraded Aladdin 2

*Chapter Four*

# *One Whale of a Storm*

*"First of all, then, I urge that supplications,
prayers, intercessions, and thanksgivings be
made for all people,"* **1 Timothy 2:1**

My father-in-law, James Nappier (whom I call Pa), and I had it made. Bobby Griffin had given us permission to hunt his old family farm in Coffee County, Georgia. He basically gave us permission to turn it into a first-class hunting preserve. We spent hundreds of hours creating shooting lanes, building shooting houses, and even converting an old, junked-up syrup-making shelter into a fully functional hunting lodge.

Every year, we shot several bucks and only one or two does. Thus our deer herd greatly increased, especially the number of harvestable bucks. We intentionally never shot any does until after Thanksgiving weekend. This allowed the bucks more opportunities to chase does during the rut (the time of year when does are in heat). Basically, when the rut starts, bucks tend to get a little stupid—more likely to blunder out into the open.

As the opening day of gun season drew near, our anticipation of the camaraderie of a great hunting season raised our excitement. That first morning we got up before dawn to get dressed and enjoy one more cup of coffee before heading to our respective hunting houses. We cautiously walked along whispering about last-minute details before splitting up.

That morning, we didn't see the first deer, but as soon as the sun rose, the neighboring hunting club started blasting away. It sounded like a full-blown war. We found out later that day that those hunters shot some nice deer.

That was just the beginning of the onslaught. Almost every time we went out, someone across the road would shoot something, usually late in the afternoon right before sunset. So that hunting season, we only killed a couple of deer.

Later we found out why our neighbors had such success. For months before and all during that hunting season, they had poured out piles of corn—literally tons of it. They basically baited the deer to their side of the road. For the deer, it was an all-you-can-eat buffet. (And for some, a last supper.)

Just one problem—baiting deer was illegal during hunting season. We were losing to outlaws. How can an honest man win out over Jesse James?

After months of disappointment, anger, and jealousy, we decided to fight back. I set out feeding corn in the spring and saw immediate results. The deer beat down the vegetation making dirt

*God is Faithful 24/7*

paths to the feeding grounds that I had created. Good thing corn was cheap at the time because the deer were eating about five hundred pounds a month.

At that time, you could feed deer in the off-season, but you had to have all of the feed cleaned up (not even one kernel left) by ten days before hunting season. One day in July, as I rode to the hunting club to put out more corn, a thought struck me: "Are you going to be legal and have all of the corn cleaned up ten days before hunting season?" I was pretty sure it was the Holy Spirit speaking to me. No, I knew it was the Holy Spirit, but wanted otherwise with all of my heart, so I embraced doubt.

The next three months, I was miserable. The question kept returning, and I remained unrepentant in my dogged determination to do it my way for the sake of prosperity. The ten-day limit before hunting season passed, and now I had committed to my iniquitous plan. During those three months, God put me on a spiritual shelf. The only light I got was the recurring question of what to do about the corn.

On October 16th, gun season loomed only three days away. At the time, I was principal at Montgomery County High School in Mt. Vernon, Georgia. After school, I drove by the house and put a hundred-pound bag of corn in the back of the truck. Self-justification required that I keep the deer drawn to our property, thus guaranteeing an awesome first day of hunting season.

*My Emmaus*

As I drove down that lonely stretch of highway, the same old question kept invading my mind. I could not deceive myself any longer. The Holy Spirit lovingly had me in His sights, and He wasn't backing down.

As I crossed the Altamaha River bridge, the conviction became unbearable. I can't really describe what happened next, but I basically exploded with emotion as I screamed a desperate prayer of forgiveness and obedience. "Father, I can't do this deed. I don't care if I ever get another deer, I will not do this thing and sin against you. Please forgive my iniquity."

I had gripped the steering wheel so hard that my hands were hurting. A few seconds after my intense repentance, I could feel the adrenalin and emotion beginning to subside. Everything seemed so surreal, and then it happened. The only thing I heard for months was the same question about what I was going to do, and now the Holy Spirit spoke two words: "Puerto Vallarta."

I immediately knew the Holy Spirit was speaking to me. Like Samuel of old, I responded, "Speak, Lord, your servant is listening." Those two words kept invading my thoughts, and then came a moment of discernment. I sensed that the Lord was asking me to intercede for the people of Puerto Vallarta.

While driving, I pleaded with God to protect the people of Puerto Vallarta. I asked him to place an invisible wall of protection around them, so that no one would be killed in that town whatever the danger may be. I went a step farther and

*God is Faithful 24/7*

rebuked the spirit of death from the people of that waterfront town. Afterward I was at total peace and completely confident in the protection of the people of Puerto Vallarta.

I continued to the hunting club. Instead of pouring out the corn I grabbed a couple of empty bags and a rake and cleaned up every kernel. Mind you, it was three days before hunting season. To be truly legal, I couldn't hunt my favorite stand for ten days. I was going to be obedient. On opening day, I hunted in a perfectly legal stand and didn't see anything.

Another week at school, and then I hit the road to be with Pa and enjoy a legal weekend of hunting in my favorite stand. The morning was still and crisply cool as the first signs of wildlife emerged — first the occasional chirping of a bird and then the scurrying of a squirrel or two. The small game made all kinds of noise, but the 150-pound, eight-point buck gracefully walked with complete stealth.

Then twenty minutes after daylight, he appeared from the early morning mist and stood majestically in the opening to my right. I admired him for several seconds before raising the barrel of my rifle. Five seconds later, my shot proved true, and now deer season had already brought success.

I had illegally schemed for something, but God took care of it when I repented and did things His way. The results of my repentance? I got a great deer, and God allowed me to know His heart and invited me to be a chosen intercessor for an entire town.

*My Emmaus*

Pa also had success that day. That weekend only added to a lifetime of memories with him.

The following Monday I came home from school, the sight of my wife overwhelmed me with joy and playful desire. I grabbed the television remote and pulled Jan into the chair with me. "Let's watch the Weather Channel, baby!"

The channel showed a video of a town that looked like a war zone. The caption at the bottom of the screen read, 'Puerto Vallarta, Mexico.'

The weatherman announced the town was hit by Hurricane Kenna, a category-five storm. Miraculously, nobody died. The hair on my neck stiffened, and a chill went down my spine. The reality of the moment excited me and induced amazement, humility, gratefulness, and praise.

I did some research on the history of Hurricane Kenna and found out that she originated from a tropical wave developing from a line of thunderstorms in the Caribbean Sea on October 16, 2002. That was the very day that the Holy Spirit broke me and asked me to intercede for the people of Puerto Vallarta.

Talk about a miracle and a life-changing lesson. Remember, I had spent three months feeling that God had put me on a shelf; there was nothing good happening spiritually that I could see. But even in my iniquity, God was developing my hunger for a renewal of righteous desire.

In reality, I had put myself on a shelf. Once I got in sync with God, He gave me one of the greatest blessings I have ever known. He used me to plead for others, and then He honored my intercessional obedience. Just think what we may have potentially missed out on as ambassadors of Christ because we haven't taken all sin seriously.

Usually the problem isn't that we can't hear or that God has quit speaking. God is simply addressing our sin, and we hear Him doing so. Until we agree and deal with that, He may not give us other orders. I encourage you, while reminding myself, to remove the seeds of iniquity from our lives. Then we will be able to hear clearly the Holy Spirit's direction. We will enrich our lives and others.

Hurricane Kenna was one whale of a storm! But in the middle of that beast, the citizens of Puerto Vallarta witnessed the grace and mercy of God. Likewise, God was precise and timely in granting me His immeasurable grace. If He had not prompted me to turn on the Weather Channel at that exact moment, I would never have known that Hurricane Kenna ever existed.

Much like a maestro flawlessly conducting an orchestra, God's grace saturated everything. You could say the same in all the particulars of your life. In the process, we all become cheerful recipients of grace and His love sings over us every minute of every day. God is gracious, and His tender mercies are everlasting!

*Chapter Five*

# You Can't Out-Give God!

> *"Will man rob God? Yet you are robbing me. But you say, 'How have we robbed you?' In your tithes and contributions. You are cursed with a curse, for you are robbing me, the whole nation of you. Bring the full tithe into the storehouse, that there may be food in my house. And thereby put me to the test, says the LORD of hosts, if I will not open the windows of heaven for you and pour down for you a blessing until there is no more need."* **Malachi 3:8-10**

Jan and I had been married about seven months, and sharing my life with such an incredible woman was beyond wonderful. Life was good, even if we barely had a penny to our name. Well, make that around 31,400 pennies ($314.00 and some change). Fortunately, we had good credit with Sears (even though we both despised debt). No money, no problem. Sears provided us with a push mower, a vacuum cleaner, and a washing machine. As I said, life was good!

*God is Faithful 24/7*

One morning, I jumped in my light blue Ford Escort and headed off to school. I got about a mile out of our driveway and suddenly saw a tan blur in my peripheral vision, then felt and heard a crash as my little car shook. Glancing in my rearview mirror, I saw a doe jump up and bound into the woods as if nothing happened.

I went back to look for evidence she had ambled off and died, but I found no blood or sign of a deer at all. That heifer had jumped up and made a clean escape. My car was not so lucky, with both passenger side doors creased severely.

When I got to school, I called the sheriff's office to report the incident. I had no reason to call the insurance company because I only had collision coverage, so I would have to pay to get it fixed. After work, I took the car to Anderson Buick Pontianc in Douglas, Georgia, for an estimate on repairing the damage.

After about ten minutes, the appraiser told me $375.00 minimum. I told them to go ahead with the repairs. Jan picked me up, and then we both started fretting about the whole ordeal.

You see, we had another account at the bank. We had not yet chosen a church home, so we set up a tithe account to deposit our first ten percent every month until we selected a church to join. Jan and I couldn't touch the account—at least, that was the plan. We have always believed that God owns everything we have, and the minimum we would give is the full tithe, or ten percent of our gross earnings.

## My Emmaus

Well, that tithe account had over $700. To pay our bill with Anderson, we decided to empty our checking account and then borrow a C-note from God. At the dealership, I was prepared to count out the entire $414 and change for the lady at the register.

She studied our paperwork. "I see that some of the material costs have actually gone down from the original estimate. So your new total will be $314." Wow, our Father loves to honor His word, right down to the penny.

As the figure settled into my mind, I couldn't contain my smile or overflowing joy. I turned and did an enthusiastic fist pump toward Jan.

I paid what we owed and put God's C-note back in my pocket. As the attendant got my car, I shared with Jan what had happened. God had plainly communicated something obvious to us. He would absolutely take care of us so we didn't have to borrow from Him. Because we were faithful to tithe, He had truly opened the windows of heaven and poured out a blessing while rebuking the devourer for us.

Soon after, we closed our tithe account and gave the proceeds to Deberry Baptist Church on the day we joined. Then Jan passed her national dental hygiene board test and started earning more than my rate as a teacher on a twelve-month contract. We were finally getting ahead financially and started saving for a house.

*God is Faithful 24/7*

A year later, Jan and I decided she should resign and look for employment elsewhere. Also, my contract had dropped to ten months, thus greatly reducing my income.

Nevertheless, we continued to pay our full tithe. We had saved about eight thousand dollars by now, so our savings could cover our financial shortfall for a while. That time was truly a test of faith, but we believed that God was able to do exceedingly, abundantly, beyond all that we could ask or imagine (Ephesians 3:20).

Jan soon found work with another dentist who had a faith like ours. She thoroughly enjoyed working with him and his team. Again, God was always at work, even when we couldn't see His hand.

Two years later, I accepted the aforementioned position as assistant principal at Irwin County High School. The first financial blessing that we got from God was cheap rent—just three hundred dollars a month in a nice home adjoining and owned by the Board of Education.

As soon as we moved in, my neat-and-all-things-ordered wife spotted all the pine straw on the roof and spent part of the next morning sweeping it off. The Superintendent of Schools, Mr. Gentry, happened to be in the parking lot observing her in amazement. I bet you he was also thinking, "What an excellent wife Mike has."

*My Emmaus*

Later that morning, Jan went to see Mr. Gentry in person to pay the rent. He commended her pine straw sweeping skills. "Since you have such initiative, let's make the first month's rent two hundred dollars instead of three." That was our first financial blessing while in Ocilla, Georgia, but many more would follow.

Not long after we arrived in Irwin County, we got to know Craig and Jonni Snyder. He was the pastor of Lighthouse Baptist Church, and one of their sons, Peter, was just starting the ninth grade. Peter and I became friends even though he was just a freshman. I considered him a role model for other students. In fact, we became so close that he would later ask me to be a groomsman in his wedding.

Shortly after meeting the Snyders, Jan and I joined their church. Right about that time, we celebrated our fourth wedding anniversary.

After that financial miracle with the blue Escort in our first year of marriage, Jan had a vision. We would own a home and pay off all debt by our fifth anniversary.

I just grinned. "You've got to be kidding."

No, she wasn't, and her faith in the matter became quite contagious.

Well, according to our schedule, that vision manifestation date loomed a little less than a year away. Our savings had continued to grow, but would there be enough to buy a home as nice as the one we were renting?

A week later, Mr. Gentry asked if we would be interested in buying our rental house, valued at $43,000.

We told him, "Absolutely!"

"Well, great then. Get back with me as soon as possible."

Jan and I prayed about how much we should offer. We decided to separately discern that amount and then compare. We had both written down $39,000. Emboldened, I relayed our offer to Mr. Gentry, who would take it to the Board's meeting the next week.

The morning after the meeting, Mr. Gentry called me to let me know that the Board would not accept any offer less than $43,000. Jan and I talked further but believed that God wanted us to stay put for now.

Two weeks later, Thony Paul, a small-town pastor from Haiti, a true Haitian nationalist, came to speak at our church. In addition to his pastoral duties, he also built and supported a school serving all the children in the surrounding communities.

Thony shared a need with Pastor Snyder—an old church that he wanted to buy in order to expand the ministry. Over the next few weeks, Thony's needs changed, and we didn't hear about it. I believed that Jan and I should give $4,000 toward the purchase of the old church.

*My Emmaus*

I relayed my desire to Jan and quickly found out we didn't agree. Remember, we were closing in on our debt-free date. The next Sunday morning at church, the Holy Spirit broke through to both of us. We went down the aisle together and with tears of conviction agreed to give the desired amount.

Craig stopped by to see us the next day. His eyes misted. "God is going to give y'all this house for $4,000 less than what the Board of Education is asking."

A couple of weeks went by, and I joined a group that flew down to Haiti to give Thony the church's gift.

We asked Thony to show us the church building he was going to buy.

He seemed confused and said he did hope to buy a particular church someday, but it was not available at the time. He really needed to immediately secure new funding for the school. Its major donor had just died.

The three of us decided to give Thony the financial gift and allow him to use it as he deemed appropriate. He was amazed at God's timing and gleefully used the money to keep the school open. Our donation was a financial miracle for the people of his town. We will never know how many children's lives we changed through continued funding of a high-quality school and staff.

Soon after returning to Georgia, I got a call from Mr. Gentry. The Board had arranged for new appraisals on the three homes

*God is Faithful 24/7*

owned by the school system. "The Chairman of the Board reaffirmed that they would not take a penny less than the appraised value."

I told him thanks and asked to know when the appraisal came in.

A couple of weeks later, Mr. Gentry called to say the appraisal for our house had come in at $39,000. I told him to make that our bid price. At the next meeting, the Board accepted our offer.

Jan and I both stood in awe at the faithfulness of God. The Holy Spirit had laid on our hearts an amount to donate to Thony that precisely matched the difference in the appraisals.

We had enough funds to buy the house, but then we would be almost broke. Needing a monetary cushion, we called Ma and Pa for a $10,000 loan until Christmas break (about six months). They agreed, and we bought the house.

In December on the day of our anniversary, we paid Ma and Pa back in person. Proud of our good stewardship, they wouldn't accept any interest. As planned, we celebrated our fifth anniversary owning our home and free of debt.

Lesson learned? Never question the vision of a godly, pretty, blue-eyed girl, and remember you can't ever out-give God. He is faithful 24/7.

*Chapter Six*

## ***Distractions***

*"But seek first the kingdom of God and his righteousness, and all these things will be added to you."* **Matthew 6:33**

Distractions, we all have had our fair share. They have been a plague on mankind ever since the serpent deceived God's faultless and flawless couple in the Garden of Eden. Distractions are designed to take our focus off what we should do and cause us to gratify our own lust or urgent desires.

Here is a classic example of how not tending the will of God can give Satan an opportunity to first attract our attention and then snare us with sin and death. King David was a man after God's own heart. I mean, if any guy ever mastered the relationship thing with God and trusted in His grace and mercy, David did. Yet David was flesh and blood like all of us, just as susceptible as any man if he lost his focus.

"In the spring of the year, the time when kings go out to battle, David sent Joab and his servants with him and all Israel. And they ravaged the Ammonites and besieged Rabbah. But David remained at Jerusalem." (2 Samuel 11:1) David was supposed to be with the army. That was his first mistake. Instead of staying focused on the needful, he focused on leisure, and it put him in the wrong place at the wrong time.

In the following verses, we see that David got up from his couch and took a stroll on his roof late one afternoon. While walking, he saw beautiful Bathsheba taking a bath.

Now much in this story we don't know. Did either of them base their decisions on the other's routine? Possibly, but we do know that David must have taken a good long look. Lust swelling in his heart resulted in a plan of action—an invitation for Bathsheba to come to the king's house.

We don't see any hesitation in her answer. Did she desire David, or did she simply obey him because he was the king? Again, we can't be sure, but she came, they lay together, and conception followed.

Shortly thereafter, Bathsheba panicked and informed David that she was pregnant. David tried to hide the infidelity. If he could get Uriah, Bathsheba's husband, to lie with her, Uriah would assume it was his baby. But Uriah, unlike David, couldn't focus on his own pleasure with so many of his countrymen fighting and dying on the battlefield. He wouldn't go along with the plan.

David finally took his scheme to another level and gave Uriah a note to deliver to General Joab. Unknowingly, Uriah carried his own death sentence.

As instructed by David, Joab placed Uriah at the front of the battle. Then Joab withdrew everyone, leaving Uriah to die.

To shorten a sad story, David takes Bathsheba to be his wife, and their child died. And now we can trace the arc; David did not focus on what he should have done, which led to distraction, which led to sin, which led to death.

Some of you might say, "I would never fall into such a trap."

Really? Let's just examine a moment in the life of good old average Joe (or Jane). He is enjoying a lovely drive down the interstate running at a cool seventy miles per hour in a three-ton SUV.

Life is grand, the leather feels good, and the climate-controlled cabin has all the comfort and convenience of first class on Emirates Air. Then he hears his favorite alert tone signaling he just received a text message. A quick, informative glance reveals it's that important text he has been waiting on all day. With little thought, he reaches for the phone and starts reading the message, then carefully glances back up at the road. It is the last thing he remembers before opening his eyes in eternity.

*God is Faithful 24/7*

Like David, instead of focusing on the needful, Joe allowed enticement to distract him. In his case, the enticement wasn't lust for his neighbor's wife but rather the addiction of social media.

What do these two stories have in common? Each distraction ended in death. Now before we castigate Joe, let's examine our own lives and see if we are guilty ourselves. Indeed, most of us have peeked at a cell phone while driving, some on a daily basis.

Thank God for his mercy and grace! But we should not put the Lord to the test. You see, I truly believe that intentional distraction while driving is just as much a sin as David's. Why? Because we are willfully putting ourselves and other drivers in great peril.

In King David and texting Joe, we see two examples of distractive activity. But literally thousands of things can serve as distractions. We must keep our focus on Jesus and learn to discern the distractions.

I spent sixteen years as a principal during my education career. I thoroughly enjoyed leading schools to higher levels of academic and extracurricular achievement. One of the things that helped me succeed as a school leader was my professional organization, the Georgia Association of Secondary School Principals (GASSP).

After my first year as principal of Montgomery County High School, I was invited to serve on the state board of directors for GASSP. I accepted the invitation and remained on the board for nine years. During that time, I moved up the ranks of leadership and ultimately sought the president-elect position.

I tried for three years. I thought I could make a difference. No, I knew I could, but my desire for the position rose from deceitful selfish ambition.

In December of 2004, I accepted an offer to become principal at Berrien High School. The next month, Melton Callahan, the executive director of GASSP, let me know that the organization had selected me as the next president-elect. I eagerly accepted; I had finally achieved my goal.

My family had moved all of our belongings into an 1100-square-foot rental house on a major thoroughfare. Single-pane windows and cramped rooms made sleeping nearly impossible.

One night that February I woke up and couldn't sleep. I lay there for a while and then got up to pray. I prayed long enough to become fully alert and enjoy my time with God.

I got quiet before the Lord, and a declarative statement came to my mind. "Father, I thank you that you have set me free from the distractions of this world!" Immediately, I heard nothing but "president-elect." My stomach sank with a sudden and sickening onslaught of anguish in my soul.

I lay there for some time trying to both hang on to my dream position and submit to God's will. A war raged within me until finally I surrendered. "I give up, Lord, I won't take this position since it's a distraction." After that, both peace and sleep returned.

*God is Faithful 24/7*

By daily practice, I got to school by 6:30 each morning. This gave me the opportunity to get things done before the interruptions started. During my first month at Berrien, no one ever showed up in my office that early.

When my alarm went off, I got ready and again arrived at school by 6:30. I had been there about five minutes with my feet propped up on my desk contemplating if I had an option, but I knew I didn't. Sometimes yielding our will to God's can be a real struggle.

At that very moment, Carol Tomberlin stepped in and leaned her hands and face against the doorpost. Now, Mrs. Tomberlin was a calculus teacher, a godly woman, and tremendous encourager whom I had come to know well my first two months at Berrien. She gave me an inquisitive look. "What are you thinking about right now?"

"Whether to accept an invitation to become president of the state principals' association."

She never moved, just gave me that broad reassuring smile. "I think God would see that as a distraction. Have a great day." She walked on down to her room.

I too finally smiled. "You win, Father, keep me focused." Later that day, I called Melton and explained why I would not be able to accept the position. I may never know what secondary and potentially life-altering distraction I may have prevented. One thing I do know is that I am exceedingly grateful for my Father's

*My Emmaus*

loving intervention and for releasing me from the stranglehold of selfish ambition.

*Chapter Seven*

## *Here Comes the Bride*

*"He who finds a wife finds a good
thing and obtains favor from
the LORD."* **Proverbs 18:22**

Queen's "Another One Bites the Dust" has been popular with sports fans for 37 years. It is a catchy little tune filled with emotion and pretty much abhorred by its intended audience of losers. Of course, they get the opportunity to return the favor to their rivals later on. Then the song goes from being abhorred to adored.

That also could define most of my dating life before marriage. As in a sporting contest, every relationship had a winner and a loser. I would break a heart, and then the next girl would crush mine. Would this cycle of despair ever cease?

It took me to age 25 to figure out what the problem was. Hey, I am a guy, and research shows that the part of the male brain that contains good judgement does not fully develop until about that age. So, there you go, scientifically speaking. To make up for our almost completely formed brain, we guys tend to favor our emotions. And in my dating experiences, one tidbit always made discernment foggy . . . the first kiss.

That first kiss always led to many more, which invariably left one or both of us seeing the relationship as more than it was. That was usually the beginning of heartbreak for somebody. The last time it happened, I hate to say, I broke the heart of a wonderful young lady; may she someday forgive me. Enough was enough! I had to do something about this insanity.

One enlightened afternoon, I promised God and myself that the next woman I kissed would be my wife. Bold, perhaps, but I knew no other way. Now, could I pull it off? I would soon find out.

Four months later, I met a charming brunette; let's call her "Tammy." We dated for nearly five weeks. Amid our holding hands and walking along a trail at Walden Lake, Tammy stopped me with a desperate question. "Mike, when are you going to kiss me?"

I told her about my promise to God.

We kept walking and holding hands. She changed our conversation to what kind of house we could have, the number of children that would be perfect for us, and so on. Wow! I remained polite and kept the date fun and upbeat.

That night, I had a detailed dream. Tammy and I were getting married in a beautifully decorated church packed with smiling and approving faces. Everything went just fine until the pastor said, "You may now kiss your bride."

I kissed her. When we turned to walk down the aisle, a wave of depression and realization settled over me. I had just married the wrong girl, and now I was stuck with her for the rest of my life.

Suddenly, I woke. The depression clung, as tangible as during the dream. Or was I dreaming? I shut my eyes tight, afraid to look around. What if I saw Tammy's face on the pillow next to me?

I finally summoned the courage to open my eyes to find myself in my own room and single. Glory hallelujah!

I experienced overwhelming relief. I appropriately broke off the relationship later that day, and we remained friends. A few months later, I started dating another charming young lady with a great sense of humor and a quick wit; let's call her "Sheila."

Coincidentally, we dated four or five weeks, and then she asked the same question of when I would kiss her. Then I gave the same answer. Even the subsequent conversation was eerily similar. We had a great date, kiss-less, and then I took her home.

That night I had the exact same dream, but I didn't wake in a panic. I opened my eyes and rolled out of bed a grateful man. I had started realizing that God would guide me precisely toward

*My Emmaus*

my wife. Later that day, I explained to Sheila that my heart was not leading me in a romantic direction with her. As in the previous relationship, we remained friends.

About that same time, I read an article by a pastor relaying the importance of praying specifically about important matters. As an example, he referred to a missionary needing a bicycle. After he started praying specifically, he miraculously received one. Instead of just verbally praying for a bike, he made a list and then prayed over it.

He specifically prayed for a blue ten-speed with a white basket on the front and a ringer on the handlebars. Well if it worked for a bicycle, it sure ought to work for a wife. So, with paper and pen in hand, I made my list of qualities, both internal and external, that I desired in my future wife.

Physically she would be about five-two, blue eyed, and brunette. I faithfully prayed over the entire list and then started thanking God for his provision and his timing.

A few months later a friend said he and his wife wanted to arrange a double date with me and a young woman they knew.

Now, I had never been on a blind date, but it sounded intriguing. "Sure thing." Like an old song this was sure enough going to be a 'first time ever I saw your face' date.

The Sunday morning before that Friday date, I pulled into the church parking lot just before the service, and another car parked next to mine. A young brunette lady got out of the car and headed toward the sanctuary.

I walked just ahead of her and sized her up at about five-two. When we got to the sanctuary, I opened the door for her and noticed her blue eyes.

"Thank you!" She then proceeded to walk to the far left side of the building.

As usual, I walked to the right side of the sanctuary and took my seat.

During the service, I kept fixating on my list of desirable wife qualities. I already knew the girl across the room met three of the requirements. Knowing that, I glanced in her direction a time or two – or three. I found out later that she did the same with me.

I was a regular attender, and this was her first visit to Emmanuel Community Baptist Church. When we got to the parking lot we exchanged names. I asked Jan if she would be returning for the evening service."

She replied yes.

"Good, I will see you tonight then."

That evening, a previously divorced couple in the church remarried, thus restoring their family. The reception was in the social hall, and Jan and I had a grand time together. We even talked politics, believe it or not.

*My Emmaus*

Sometimes you hear people describe a successful date by saying, "We closed the place down." Well, Jan and I closed the church down that night. Our conversation continued into the parking lot, and we were the last two to leave.

Before we left, I asked for her phone number. Amazingly bold of me, but she let me have it.

Now, remember, in five days I had a blind date with this same young lady. Coincidence? I don't think so. Not so blind after all!.

We all had a great time, and the courtship began. Jan and I started seeing each other several times a week. After five weeks, I realized that with her, I could check off every box on my list of desirable qualities.

Jan and I had fun bowling with friends one evening, and then I took her home. When I walked her to the steps of her back door, she took one step up and turned. This brought us eye to eye.

Immediately, I saw it as clearly as if she had a neon sign flashing, "This is your wife!"

Blown away, I realized I had a decision to make. Would I kiss my wife at that moment or wait until we walked the aisle? I chose the former, and we have been kissing for over thirty years now!

Not only did I get a great gal, but I became great friends with her mom and dad. About nine months after we started dating, Jan moved to Tallahassee to attend dental hygiene school. The miles couldn't separate us; we both knew our engagement was coming.

First, though, I would need a ring. At the time, I had no savings, just a $630 income tax refund check. While driving down a remote country road, I wondered, "How can I afford a ring worthy of the girl of a lifetime on $630?"

Startling me from my thoughts, a Toyota Celica flew around me, and the driver eagerly honked the horn. Inside were my friends Charlie and Jeannie, who lived over an hour away.

He motioned for me to pull over, so I did. The three of us embraced and exchanged excited, heartfelt greetings.

Charlie then asked, "Mike, what were you thinking when we came around you?" I shared my burden with them, and Charlie just smiled broadly and chuckled. "Problem solved. I broker diamonds, and for you I have the perfect ring in mind."

He gave me a ridiculous deal: exchanging my refund check for a truly flawless half-carat diamond ring. I owe them forever for their gracious generosity.

God truly knows what we need before we even call. Precisely while the prayer formulated in my mind, He brought Charlie and Jeannie by. Yes, God really is in the details of our lives, and as the apostle Paul states in Ephesians 3:20, "He is able to do exceedingly, abundantly, beyond all that we can ask or imagine."

*My Emmaus*

A couple of months later, I asked Jan to marry me during a sunset at Bradenton Beach, Florida. She agreed, so I excitedly slipped the ring on her finger. That flawless ring was even more beautiful than I had imagined. We admired its twinkling rainbow colors in the fading sunlight.

Thirteen months later, we walked down the aisle and into a new life together. I should take this moment to encourage single readers to remain virgins until marriage. I cannot describe the joy of giving each other the perfect gift of purity on our honeymoon night.

However, if, like the great majority who have stumbled, you find yourself not able to give such a gift, or you are now married and wasn't able to present that gift, then trust in the restorative grace of God that comes through repentance and forgiveness. Next, choose to be committed to your spouse and stay faithful to him or her from this day forward. Remember, joy is just one of the many rewards of being faithful.

*Chapter Eight*

## *Freedom from Fear and the Warrior's Armor*

*"Finally, be strong in the Lord and in the strength of his might."* **Ephesians 6:10**

Fred was back in his home country as a new creation, and our first son was now six months old. Jake, the first baby born to our new congregation, affectionately became known as "the church baby," a masterful piece of God's work.

I truly had a greater appreciation for the full meaning of God's word—in particular, Psalm 139:14: "I praise you, for I am fearfully and wonderfully made. Wonderful are your works; my soul knows it very well." In the previous eighteen months God taught me so much and showed His strength on my behalf. Even so, my path would veer into the dark valley of despair.

I believe it was the third week of January, 1996. In the hall at school, I felt a piercing pain in my side. It stopped me briefly and then subsided quickly, so I continued. A few minutes later, it happened again and subsided just as quickly. It was unlike any

*My Emmaus*

twinge of pain I had ever experienced before. Later that day, it happened again.

Then at my desk, I considered the random thought: "You have cancer!" I shook it off and continued to work. Within a couple of minutes, the thought returned.

I failed to realize that the battle had already begun, and the weapons of my warfare lay scattered on the ground around me, completely useless. Why? You can't wear what you haven't put on. The more the thought persisted, the more ensnared I became as an ignorant casualty of the unseen war raging around me. I was like a Roman soldier walking into battle armed only with a tunic.

Ephesians 6 should be near the top of every believer's list of scriptures to memorize, digest, and activate. Verses 10-20 give us a descriptive and practical view of how to engage in combat with the enemy of our souls.

After a restless night's sleep, I woke the next morning to have my quiet time. It is Usually a wonderful interlude, but the thoughts of the previous day returned with a vengeance. I put up an anemic defense and fell to defeat before I ever left the house.

The rest of the day, I tried to think on positive things, but the same despairing thought kept returning to kick me in my mental and emotional gut. By evening, I felt physically and spiritually exhausted. Moreover, the battle had just begun.

This mundane, beaten-down existence carried on for over a week. No matter how hard I prayed, I couldn't find relief. Sometime during that second week, that repetitive invading thought expanded in scope and brought a few more along with it, compounding my devastating discouragement. "The cancer is going to get you, and you'll be gone." That was the worst blow yet, and more would follow.

That thought expanded to truly destroy me when it saturated my mind as, "Another man is going to marry Jan and raise your son." Three weeks of this moved me further into the grip of fear and despair. No matter how much I called out to God, relief was nowhere to be found. Sometimes I could only say, "Dear Jesus!" Through the silence I persisted in prayer and held on to shoestring like hope.

We read in scripture that Daniel fasted 21 days while waiting for God to answer. Daniel didn't know God had heard him from day one and that the answer was already on the way. Between his initial prayer and receiving the answer, Daniel had God's two most prominent angels engaged in spiritual warfare on his behalf. Gabriel fought with the unseen spiritual "Prince of Persia." Michael arrived and freed Gabriel to deliver the message.

My situation was much like Daniel's. God had heard my prayers, and warfare raged on.

During the fourth week of the enemy's unrelenting campaign of terror, a teacher called me and asked if I would come to her room to get a student.

"Sure thing." I took off down the hall. Along the way, the mocking thoughts came at me like heavy hail in a thunderstorm. They undermined my concentration so much that I had to stop halfway to her room.

Where was I going? What was I supposed to be doing? I leaned against the wall and racked my brain for at least a minute before I finally knew my destination and purpose again.

I managed to do my job the rest of the day, but I could no longer hide this struggle's effects. The week had ended, and I faced Sunday morning. Soon I would have to lead praise and worship again.

I felt like such a hypocrite struggling to do what should have been a real joy. Especially leading everyone in the "happy-clappy" songs we so loved to do. As we transitioned from praise and worship to the sermon, I sat beside my wife on the sofa nearest the front.

During the service, I noticed Melvin writing on a yellow piece of paper and putting it in his bible. Melvin was a dear brother in the Lord, a true role model for all of us men. We all affectionately called him "Sweet Melvin."

When Craig finished his sermon, he brought us to our feet and prayed a benediction to close the service.

Melvin quickly spoke up. "Craig, we can't leave yet, the Holy Spirit isn't through."

"What is it, Melvin?"

"Someone here thinks they have cancer. Who are you?"

Stunned, I stood dead silent.

After what seemed like a minute, Melvin asked again, "Someone thinks they have cancer, who are you?"

I finally raised my hand. "It's me!"

Immediately, Jan slapped the couch seat. "I knew it!"

Craig and Melvin then asked me to sit in a chair in front of the pulpit.

All the men in the room gathered around me to place their hands on me and pray. They took turns praying that God would strengthen me and free me from my unseen enemy. Melvin rebuked the spirit of fear and commanded it to cease ministering to me. Then they all started praising God.

All I can tell you is that a month of mental and emotional hell on earth vanished. I felt unbelievably clean and refreshed.

After everyone had left, Melvin handed me his yellow paper. He'd written Ephesians 6:10 across the top with the following message: "This attack is a scheme of the evil one. It is a scare tactic to destroy your ministry for Jesus. Jesus has heard your prayers; he knows your concern about this matter. You do not have cancer. This is a spiritual battle. You are being ministered to by a spirit of fear."

That morning filled me with awe, yet more would come that evening. What a refreshing day I'd had. That night, after the church service, Craig asked me to stay and meet with him and one of the ladies of our congregation.

They shared with me something that only they and her nine-year-old son knew. The young boy had just gotten saved a couple of months earlier. The previous Sunday, which began my fourth week of spiritual attack, the boy leaned over and said, "Mama, there is a demon behind Mr. Parker."

She brushed him off. "Shush, be quiet."

A minute later, he pulled her sleeve. "Mama, the demon behind Mr. Parker knows I can see it."

That evening, she mentioned it to Craig. They both took it into confidence. The gravity of the situation blew us all away. God had allowed me to endure an incredible onslaught of the enemy, revealed it to the eyes of a young boy, and then confirmed it through Melvin.

Some of you may now be thinking this is all crazy.

Really? What if I told you it was scriptural? The Bible records such an incident in 2 Kings 6:17. In this scripture we see the

Prophet Elisha standing in an encampment with a young lad riddled with fear at the enormity of their fleshly enemy.

In response, Elisha prayed. "O LORD, please open his eyes that he may see." So God opened his eyes, and "behold, the mountain was full of horses and chariots of fire all around Elisha." God allowed the lad to see that in the spirit world, real warfare goes on unseen around us, and that greater are they who are with us than they who are against us.

Yes, we have a real enemy, and we tend to not think about what goes on in the unseen world around us. However, we shouldn't be ignorant, complacent, or ill prepared for the fiery darts of the evil one. That is why God gave us the breastplate of righteousness, the belt of truth, the shoes of the gospel of peace, the helmet of salvation, the shield of faith, and the sword of the spirit. Each piece serves a specific purpose.

The shield of faith would have quenched those fiery missiles that the enemy shot into my mind. Likewise, the sword of the Spirit would have annihilated the first lying thought lobbed my way.

If I had hidden 2 Corinthians 10:4-5 in my heart, I would have known exactly how to respond to Satan's clever scheme. "For the weapons of our warfare are not of the flesh but have divine power to destroy strongholds. We destroy arguments and every lofty opinion raised against the knowledge of God, and take every though captive to obey Christ."

*My Emmaus*

Oh, I had memorized that verse, but I needed to meditate on it to really know how to use it effectively and to have it in the forefront of my mind.

God gives us in nature a perfect model of meditating on His word. We see it revealed in the rudimentary habits of cattle.

Picture a cow chewing the cud. I hate to be graphic, but it will help you understand the analogy. Unlike humans, a cow has a four-compartmented stomach. This setup allows a cow to fill up on grasses and grains and then relax under a shade tree. There she regurgitates the swallowed food (the "cud") back up into her mouth.

Then the cow re-chews in order to break it down further. This process allows the cow to extract more of the nutrients from the grasses and grains. This regurgitation repeats several times and ultimately makes the cow more efficient in turning carbohydrate energy into meat and milk.

Likewise, we become spiritually sharp when we meditate on the word of God prayerfully mulling it over in our mind and, thus truly internalizing it.

After that eventful Sunday, I returned to work energized, rested, and ready to go.

A math teacher, Colonel Jim Allison, U.S. Army retired, came by my office to say he couldn't teach his group of young men at the youth correctional facility that evening. Would I mind

*God is Faithful 24/7*

teaching for him? Cecil Burkett would be there to play the guitar and help with any ministry needs if I would bring the message.

I asked if he had a curriculum.

"Just whatever the Lord gives you!"

I thanked him for the opportunity. I prayed that the Lord would bless me with just the right message and then moved on with my plentiful assistant principal work.

At the correctional facility that evening, the officer on duty announced that our group would arrive in a minute. Then added that another group leader wasn't going to make it and asked if I would take both groups. And by the way, each group represents one hundred teenage boys.

I smiled. "Sure, the more the merrier."

Somehow, we crammed all two hundred into one room. Cecil did a great job with the music, and then I brought a message about the life of Joseph, sold into slavery and then cast into prison for doing the right thing. I talked about how Joseph made the most of his time. God kept elevating him until he became second-in-command in all of Egypt. I then related Joseph's experience to theirs and to the gospel.

For fifteen minutes they sat dead silent, and all two hundred sets of eyes followed my every move. Obviously, the Holy Spirit had moved and grabbed their undivided attention.

At the end of the service I asked, "If anyone knows beyond doubt that God is dealing with you about being saved, stand up and be ready to give your heart to Christ."

One hundred teenagers immediately stood. I led them in a prayer of salvation and then had each come forward and provide their name and home phone number for future contact.

It remains the single most fruitful ministry experience of my life thus far. Melvin was right on target; Jesus had a ministry for me, and the enemy had tried to destroy it.

Yes, spiritual warfare is real, and even though this is not intended to be a manual on spiritual warfare, perhaps it has interested you enough to learn more regarding this most important topic.

Satan doesn't fight fair, and nor does he take the battle for granted. Neither should we. You have witnessed in this chapter a practical experience of real spiritual warfare. Our unseen adversaries will always return, so be on the alert. Remember, after Satan tempted Jesus in the wilderness, he departed until an opportune time.

When that opportune time arrives for you, your response must be like the Apostle Paul's and an untold host of saints, present and past. We must fight on and keep standing, fully girded with the armor of God.

*Chapter Nine*

# *Fasting for Children – Part Two*

*And in due time Hannah conceived and bore a son, and she called his name Samuel, for she said, "I have asked for him from the Lord."* **1 Samuel 1:20**

I had spent over 27 years of my education career at the high school level. Fourteen of those I served as a high school principal. For the last two years of my career, I had the opportunity to hang out with the little people of education as a primary school principal.

Every day was one big affirmation after another. I loved my kids, and my kids loved me. Who couldn't look forward to a couple hundred hugs a day? And I mean that literally!

As one of the largest primary schools in the state, we had fourteen hundred students in kindergarten through third grade. One day in early October, 2014, I went down the hall first thing in the morning to check all of the duty posts. As I approached the

*My Emmaus*

entrance to the kindergarten wing, I could see Jessica standing in her normal place.

In many ways, she reminded me of my wife—petite, brunette and full of life. Usually Jessica had a beautiful smile and infectious personality, but today from fifty feet away I could see her great emotional distress. I greeted her with "Good morning."

She stayed quiet with quivering lips.

I drew closer. "Jessica, are you all right?"

Again, she couldn't verbally reply. She shook her head several times, affirming her poor spirits.

I asked if she would speak with one of our other speech therapists.

Again she shook her head no.

Then I asked if she needed to take the day off.

She nodded yes.

The other two speech therapists were each old enough to be Jessica's mom. They both treated her like a daughter. Immediately they shifted into mama mode to assist her in getting her things together and making sure she got home safely. They also checked on her throughout the day.

The next morning, to my immediate relief, I saw Jessica at her duty station as usual. We exchanged greetings, and then I prepared to verbalize a question that had preoccupied my thoughts for the past twelve hours.

"Jessica, may I ask you a personal question?"

"Yes, Sir."

"Your great distress yesterday—did it have anything to do with not being able to have children?" Odd question, I know. I just asked what I felt the Lord leading me to ask. I didn't even know if she and husband Lee wanted children.

Jessica teared up, lips quivering again. "Yes, Sir, absolutely." She and Lee had in fact been trying to conceive for some time.

I gave her a hug and asked her to come see me sometime that day when she had a few minutes.

She agreed and showed up about mid-morning in my office. We took a seat at the table, and I told her how twenty years before, I fasted and prayed three days for the Lord to heal Jan and I so that we could have children (see chapter two). I believed the time had come for fasting for children–part two.

"Jessica, the Lord is leading me to fast and pray for three days and then anoint you and Lee with oil to conceive and bring forth a child. Is that something that you want me to do?"

"Yes!" She promised to consult with Lee and let me know.

A week went by, and I hadn't heard anything from Jessica, so I stepped to her office to check. She said that she and Lee both wanted me to fast and pray. I agreed to fast Sunday night through 4 p.m. Wednesday, when I'd meet them in my office for anointing and praying.

You need to know that most of the time fasting isn't very fun. But I have found that something about the whole fasting process brings humility and builds faith. This particular fast breezed by the first two days.

At the end of day two, I felt led to read a certain devotion on crosswalk.com, not knowing it concerned Hannah and Samuel. In 1 Samuel 1, we find that Hannah married a godly man named Elkanah. Elkanah actually had two wives, Peninnah and Hannah. You could say Peninnah was the baby mama because she didn't have any problem getting pregnant and bearing sons and daughters for Elkanah. Yet Hannah, whom he dearly loved, remained barren year after year.

To worsen Hannah's misery, Peninnah, would mock Hannah for her barrenness during their annual pilgrimages to the tabernacle. Hannah's grief deepened year after year. Finally, Hannah prayed intently that the Lord would give her and Elkanah a son. She even promised to present the child to the Lord after weaning. The Lord heard her cry and opened her womb so she could conceive. As a result, Hannah gave birth to Samuel.

The devotion focused on Hannah crying out to God. My excitement soared. God had confirmed to me that He would give

Jessica and Lee a son. I couldn't wait to anoint them and pray, but I still had almost 24 hours to fast and pray before doing so.

That last day of fasting challenged me greatly. I knew the enemy wanted to sidetrack me, but I endured until Jessica and Lee showed up. When they arrived, I shared the previous night's confirming devotion. Both beamed with uncontained joy and expectation.

I anointed them and prayed as planned, then laughed and told them to go home and enjoy a long weekend together. I couldn't wait to witness the outcome.

Less than a month, Jessica stopped by my office squealing with delight. You guessed it—she was pregnant! Moreover, according to her test, she conceived during that long weekend, less than five days after I'd completed the fast. Hallelujah!

The next eight months and a week, Jessica got the full spectrum of pregnancy's great joys and challenges. Yes, she experienced great nausea—and not just in the mornings, bless her. But finally little Henry arrived.

Their amazing boy loves praise and worship songs and just brims with joy. His name may be Henry, but we believe Jessica and Lee have a little Samuel in the making.

I now believe more than ever that a little fasting with your praying can and will do immense good. Besides, after you complete a fast, the taste and textures of food always seem to tantalize and satisfy even more. So enjoy the fruits of your fasting and the richness of God's bounty, and in the words of Iron Chef Alton Brown, "Good eats!"

*Chapter Ten*

# *God Is Faithful 24/7*

*'If we are faithless, he remains faithful – for he cannot deny himself.'* **2 Timothy 2:13**

The previous and following chapters are descriptive narratives of some of my most favorite personal Emmaus moments. But before any of these events came the journey of my own salvation. It too may be unique, but I feel that many of you can relate to portions of it. Likewise, all of us should agree that the sinner has nothing to do with his own salvation except to attest that he is a sinner in need of a savior. By His grace, He takes us as we are and makes us His own.

My mom and dad raised us (three boys, one girl) as God-fearing regular churchgoers at Welcome Baptist Church. We knew where we would be on Sunday morning, Sunday evening, and Wednesday night—at church with many of our friends.

*My Emmaus*

Sundays were always special in the Parker household. In addition to church, it almost always included lunch with Granny and Grandpa and usually a backyard football game in the neighborhood. Church provided other meeting opportunities. Several miles down the road, my uncle served as an awesome pastor at Lone Oak Baptist church. When I was nine, Uncle Buddy had a guest evangelist, "Reverend Wood." Our family loaded up in the station wagon one night and made the quick trip to Lone Oak.

I can't remember the subject of the sermon, just that it brought streams of tears down my face. At the end of the service, Wood gave an altar call.

My dad leaned over and asked if I wanted to go down front.

"Yes, Sir!"

Down front, Wood asked if I wanted to get saved.

Again, my favorite phrase for the evening gushed out, "Yes, Sir!"

When the music stopped, Wood announced, "We have a young boy accepting Jesus as his savior tonight."

Everyone clapped and said amen, and then we all went home.

Here's the thing, though. Neither Wood nor anyone else at the altar ever counseled with me or led me in a prayer of salvation. I was just a young boy under conviction and knew I needed a savior.

A few weeks later, I got baptized in the Alafia river. Now, maybe God honored my desire for salvation when I humbly walked down the aisle that night, but for certain, I always had doubts about my salvation. At age sixteen I got baptized again, but often the doubts would return.

When I got out of college, I often listened to WCIE, a Christian contemporary radio station out of Lakeland, Florida. I also played Candy Hemphill, Amy Grant, and Sandi Patti albums through my headphones every night. I would just lie there listening and deep down yearn for absolute certainty in my standing with Jesus.

This was the early 1980s. Cold War tensions raged between the United States and Soviet Union, and fears of nuclear war kept many up at night. When I least expected, my life could end in a billion-degree flash of radiation—then what would become of my soul?

My family owned an agricultural publication business that my dad ran out of our house. One day, I was home alone typing advertising invoices. Suddenly I broke down sobbing uncontrollably. I cried out to God, "Lord, heal me or take me home."

I knew I had to get out of the house, so I decided to ride out to Steppin' Stone Farm Girls Home to mow the pasture. I volunteered sometimes at this Christian home for troubled girls (runaways, delinquents, addicts, and the severely disobedient).

*My Emmaus*

I climbed into the cab of my pickup truck. That day, November 20, 1983, was quite cool both in and out of my truck, but not for long.

Still wiping away tears, I felt as if someone placed a warm blanket around me. Though physically alone, I was not alone spiritually. The Holy Spirit had gotten into that truck with me. Actually, he was always present, but now I was aware of his all-embracing love.

As I drove to the farm, I reflected on the past twenty minutes. Once there, I cranked up the tractor. As I mowed the pasture, I was half-thinking and half-crying out to God. His presence was still very real to me.

Then I sensed the Lord saying, "Now, Mike, now is the time to nail down your salvation."

I got off the tractor and left it running as I kneeled and cried out to God, "Lord Jesus, I know that I am a sinner. Your word is plain about that fact. I believe that you were born to the Virgin Mary, lived a sinless life, and as both God and man died on the cross for my sins. I believe that you rose from the grave after three days and that presently you are sitting at the right hand of the Father interceding for me. Jesus, I am tired of living my life my way, now I want you to live your life through me. Please forgive me and be the Lord of my life. Thank you for forgiving me and saving me."

When I finished praying, one verse came to my mind, Luke 15:10: "Just so, I tell you, there is joy before the angels of God over one sinner who repents."

I continued to pray, "Father, I know the angels in heaven are now rejoicing because I have finally made it home." Relieved, I stood at peace with God. Whatever happened to my physical body, my soul belonged to Him.

That very night, The Day After premiered on television. The movie depicted the day that the Russians launched hundreds of missiles at America and within minutes blew most us away. We saw Americans suffering from homelessness, starvation, and the horrendous effects of nuclear fallout.

Any other time, it would have petrified me, but that night I went to bed without any fear, full of joy because I was saved. Before going to sleep, I read the first chapter of John, and the words for the first time seemed to come alive: "In the beginning was the Word, and the Word was with God, and the Word was God. He was in the beginning with God. All things were made through him, and without him was not anything made that was made. In him was life, and the life was the light of men." (John 1:1-5) I had the life of Christ!

That night, sleep came quickly and peacefully. About two months later, I went to work at Steppin' Stone Farm as a full-time missionary. As a staff member, I performed maintenance, tended the grounds, and supervised the agricultural activities of the farm.

Working at the farm was a constant job, and I was the only guy there. I hit a spiritual rough spot about a year into my missionary service and fell into deep, dark depression.

During my descent, I started thinking that I had lost my salvation or maybe never had it, and now I had lost my chance. It was a dark pit, but my savior proved much more tenacious than any valley of despair. He loved me out of the darkness and back to the realization of His warm embrace. You see, for Him the dark valley was as light as noon without any shadows.

I fully came to understand and cherish 2 Timothy 2:13: "If we are faithless, he remains faithful–for he cannot deny himself." One day while still on my way out of the dark valley, I rode in my truck listening to WCIE when the radio host said, "I feel impressed to share this with someone who is in a dark place. The Lord wants you to know and embrace 1 John 3:20: 'For whenever our heart condemns us, God is greater than our heart, and he knows everything.'"

I knew that the Lord was using this individual to speak life to my soul. Immediately, I felt refreshed, and the burden lifted. Now the valley didn't seem so dark and deep.

A couple of days later, I had breakfast with a pastor friend. Terry, a real joy to be with, offered great encouragement to others.

While we ate, he paused and said that he believed the Lord wanted me to focus on one verse of scripture, "though my heart condemns me, God is greater than my heart and knows all things." Deep down, I had to chuckle.

Through that dark valley, my gentle shepherd loved me and led me out of the darkness. Maybe you have dealt with some of those same fears. You may think you've blown it so badly you can never have peace with God. Or maybe you're ready to give up because everything's just too hard. The fact that you are still reading this book proves beautifully that the Lord still ministers His grace to you.

Remember, some of God's greatest saints, like Elijah and John the Baptist, know how the dark valley can cause anguish and doubt. God led them out of the valley, and He stands ready to do the same for everyone that may know it's companionship. I don't care what the obstacle or unseen foe, you are not alone, and God's all-embracing love is available for you. Believe it! Receive it! For it is a fact!

God has promised us in Ephesians 3:20 that He is able to do exceedingly abundantly above all that we ask or think, according to the power that works in us (NKJV). May we be like King David continually understanding that God is with us in the valley to comfort us, protect us, and lead us out! That said, I must share another dark valley with you or I would have to consider this book incomplete.

About nine years ago, I sensed I should speak to the man that owned the vacant house behind us. He lived in the same county,

## My Emmaus

but I didn't know where. My neighbor advised me to reconsider trying to see him because the guy was crazy.

A couple of weeks later, I felt like I should see him by Thanksgiving, but I didn't follow through. Five days after that, a friend came over to help me build my storage shed. He told me, "You know, the old guy who owned the house behind you shot and killed himself on Thanksgiving."

In a rush of anger and despair, I threw my hammer against the wall of my shed. "I was supposed to go see him by Thanksgiving!" I couldn't bear the grief. Once again, even though the valley loomed deep and dark, the same loving God that I disobeyed led me through and out of the darkness.

Three years after that failure, I took my youngest, Ben, to lunch at Cracker Barrel. Ben finished eating and moved over to the checkerboard table. No matter the outcome of the game, Ben would win; he was playing against himself.

I continued to eat my lunch and watch Ben in amusement. A thought came from nowhere: "Tell these people how much I love them." Immediately, I was both amazed and appalled. Again, the thought came clearly and tenderly: "Tell these people how much I love them."

I prayed, "No, Lord. Anything but this."

*God is Faithful 24/7*

The thought returned with greater clarity and compassion. "Remember the neighbor who killed himself on Thanksgiving? Tell these people how much I love them."

I didn't need any further motivation. Suddenly I knew the overwhelming emotions that Peter must have experienced after denying the Lord three times.

I knew that God wanted to demonstrate His love to those present, and some of them were likely in a desperate state. Emboldened with an overwhelming desire to be faithful, I swallowed my fear, took a deep breath, and stood. "May I have your attention, please?"

The whole restaurant, though packed, got completely silent.

"Look around us at all of this abundance. We as a nation and a people are truly blessed with more than enough, and on top of all this, Jesus stretched out his arms on the cross." I stretched out my arms likewise. "He said, 'I love you this much.' God bless each and every one of you." Then I took my seat and worked on completing my meal.

In a minute or so, two older women stopped by my table and thanked me for my boldness. I thanked them, and they left the restaurant.

Shortly after that, a young man came over and asked if he could sit.

"Sure, have a seat."

*My Emmaus*

"Sir, I have never seen such a bold witness for Christ in all of my life. I am a state FFA officer, and tonight I am responsible for giving the blessing at the state livestock show banquet. There will be over a thousand adults, FFA, and 4-H members present. After what you've done at lunch today I am encouraged to be as bold."

"Praise God, just make sure you bless the meal in the name of Jesus."

He said he would, and later that evening he did.

After he left, several other people stopped by to thank me. In the process, I went through Peter's transition. I had experienced the emotions of Peter's failures after denying Christ three times. Now I had risen to Peter's restoration, when Jesus asked him three times, "Peter, do you love me?"

After each question, Peter replied, "Lord, you know that I love you."

Jesus gave follow-up commands: "Feed my sheep" and "Tend my lambs."

God used Peter mightily the rest of his life. Likewise, that day was a restoration of sorts for me. Even though fear had gripped my heart, I stepped out in faith, and that act of obedience made a clear difference to several people — and probably more.

I believe someone in the restaurant that day had thoughts of suicide. Maybe he/she/they now live safe in Christ instead of the alternative.

I may never know the full fruit of that act of obedience this side of heaven, but one day I will. In the meantime, may we all remember daily that God is faithful 24/7.

*Chapter Eleven*

# A Wolf in Sheepdog's Clothing

*'Do not be deceived: "Bad company ruins good morals"'* **1 Corinthians 15:33**

Patch was our family dog and a wonderful best friend to my boys, Jake and Ben. Playful and beautiful, she brimmed with energy. In fact, you could call her perfect, unmatched in her devotion and just an overall joy.

She loved to play next door and in our yard with Shady, the neighbors' chocolate Lab. Oh, Patch's breeding? Border collie. This particular breed has for centuries herded sheep, and they go at it all day with overflowing genetic joy. What do I mean by genetic? Many domesticated pets are the result of years of selective breeding to genetically develop the traits desired. When successfully accomplished, it can and should bring about tremendous satisfaction and great results.

Raising children can be a lot like that. Not that we can choose what traits we want in a child (although that's becoming possible), but we should be able to train a child in the way he or she should go. More on that later.

When we manipulate genetics through breeding, we sometimes encounter a sudden regression. This is a hidden, undesired trait that some outside influence can activate.

In Patch's case, she and her pal, Shady, unbeknownst to us, had become friends with a pit bull/boxer. Now, this mix also has certain inbred traits, specifically an aggressive and fearless demeanor. One Friday night, Patch and Shady decided to embrace the tendencies of their new running buddy and whole-heartedly regressed a few thousand years.

This marvel of a sheepdog and goat herder joined in on a frenzied all-night killing spree. In a matter of hours, Patch rejected all her ancestors' disciplined breeding and became a wolf in sheepdog's clothing.

I learned this from a neighbor across the branch, Bud Brantley. He came breathless to my house early one Saturday morning and through desperate gasps managed to say, "Your dog, Mike, your dog! Patch and Shady and a pit bull are killing my goats!"

Stunned, I didn't know what to say. I got in the truck with Bud, and we drove over to his house. The sight sickened me. They had mauled three goats to death and severely injured four more. I could only imagine the pain and fear those goats experienced during the night.

I got home to find Patch there. By personality, she seemed to be the same old Patch, but we could not deny the evidence.

I met with the owners of Shady and the pit bull. We three agreed that we could never trust our supposedly tame pets again. We did what we had to do and got rid of our pets. Now for the double shock. Bud's goats were no ordinary livestock but rather championship Boer show goats.

The insurance adjuster estimated their worth at over fifty thousand dollars. What? The three of us pet dads committed to making things right with Bud, but first we would check with our insurance companies to see what they could do for us.

At home in the living room, Jan and I discussed the potentially exasperating cost of our dogs' actions with Wade (Shady's owner and our neighbor). Jake, then seven years old, must have heard us. With tears streaming down his face, he slinked into the room and stammered, "Will this help?"

He held up a rattlesnake skin wallet that Papa made for him. Jake kept it in his dresser drawer and filled it with every dollar he'd ever received.

Immediately, my heart sank. Moved to tears, I grabbed him in a big hug and told him to keep his money because everything would be all right. Then I just kept loving on him. My eyes are welling up again now just writing about it.

Our share of the reparation would have been about $18,500 — heartbreaking. Fortunately, all three insurance companies paid up, and Jan and I owed nothing. What a relief to have someone else step in and pay the debt in full!

You know someone else once and for all paid a debt that would have perpetually broken your heart and mine throughout eternity. His name is Jesus. Yes, he paid our debt in full, and if we will believe that with all of our hearts and ask for His forgiveness, He will forgive us and set us free to live and reign with him.

Well, that day stressed us greatly, but God would end it in a truly special way. That evening Jan and I gathered our young boys around us to further comfort them and to teach the lesson that God wanted them to learn. I told Jake and Ben, "Boys, Patch was bred and raised to look after livestock and to protect them from predators, but today she and her buddy, Shady, got to running with a dog of questionable character. They followed his lead and started harassing goats. With the first taste of blood, they became enraged killers.

"Guys, you can do everything right as a parent, raise your children to be loving and kind, to not steal or kill, and to avoid hanging around questionable characters. But ultimately God has given each of us a free will. With that, we can embrace the wonderful life that God wants to give us, or we can choose to go down a different road that leads to destruction. We need to learn

*My Emmaus*

from Patch that she chose destruction. May none of us ever follow such a path. May we wholeheartedly follow Jesus."

God took a stressful, painful experience, especially for Jake and Ben, and made something good out of something bad. A father and mother got a chance to make one of life's dark valleys into an extraordinary teachable moment bathed in the light and love of Christ.

*Chapter Twelve*

# *A Bad Case of Déjà vu*

*"For he will command his angels concerning you to guard you in all your ways. On their hands, they will bear you up, lest you strike your foot against a stone."*
**Psalm 91:11-12**

As the psalmist said, "We are fearfully and wonderfully made." The design and function of our bodies, our ability to think and reason, and even the engagement of our emotions truly amaze us. Our Creator, Jesus, really did save the best for last. Now, I know a lot of quick-thinking women out there would eagerly agree with that statement. After all, Eve came last in His creative designs.

Well, you won't get any argument from me. After over thirty years with Jan, I agree. Everything about her awes me, as if she came straight from God's original blueprints.

The boys and I have learned to appreciate Jan's discernment and listen to her wise counsel. Likewise, I have lost track of the times that my own mother's wisdom and discernment kept us kids from physical, mental and emotional harm.

You see, a discerning woman makes a praying woman, and a praying woman leads to a lifetime of benefits for those in her loving crosshairs. How does all of this relate to déjà vu? Well, I am glad you asked?

Sometimes we may repeatedly think about something, and then one day out of the randomness of life, the stars line up and that thought process shows up in living color. That happened with a scenario that had played out in my mind several times ever since I first got my driver's license. I must have visualized the following scenario at least ten times.

I am driving down a two-lane road and approaching a bridge. A slow-moving semi-truck comes across the bridge in the oncoming lane. Suddenly a speeding car whips out from behind the truck, trying to pass it in my lane. I have nowhere to go.

I visualized the total hopelessness of the situation, the complete lack of control, the emotional shock, and then the finality of such an incident. Yet by wasting so much mental energy on picturing that scenario, I had completely defied the reality of Psalm 91.

No situation is hopeless when God gets involved, and He watches over even the smallest detail. In Psalm 91:11-12, we see that God has commanded his angels concerning us to guard us in all of our ways, and that on their hands they will bear us up, lest we strike our foot against a stone. During those daydreams I should have envisioned God's angels coming to my rescue and doing what seemed impossible.

You see, what we think about is vitally important. Paul tells us God's answer to worthless thinking in Philippians 4:8, "Finally, brothers, whatever is true, whatever is honorable, whatever is just, whatever is pure, whatever is lovely, whatever is commendable, if there is any excellence, if there is anything worthy of praise, think about these things." Do these words in any way describe what I had been visualizing? Absolutely not!

Now I am not saying that we should not visualize potential dangers altogether. Sometimes that allows God to turn His creative wisdom loose in our minds to correct hazardous situations. But, I don't believe we should repeatedly visualize a hopeless scenario and then keep it hopeless in our minds.

Worse, I even shared the semi-truck/car scenario with a friend. At that point, the enemy of my soul became aware of my fear. I can safely say that you should keep some things unsaid.

Well, let's get back to a praying woman and tie these two thoughts together. Soon after getting engaged, Jan and I had an in-home date with her parents. After I arrived at their house, a heavy rain started. According to the weatherman, this steady downpour would continue throughout the night.

Later that evening, I decided to make the ten-minute trek back to my house. Ma grabbed me by the arm and asked me not to

## My Emmaus

go. Gravely concerned about me driving in that rain, she insisted that I spend the night. I told her I would be fine, but she persisted.

Finally, looking a little unnerved, she let me leave. She asked me to call her when I got home. As I walked out the door, she immediately started praying for my safety.

The short walk to my car got me soaking wet. Man, was it coming down!

I was two miles from home and approaching the Alafia River bridge when the unthinkable—or should I say my thinkable thing—happened. A semi-truck was in the oncoming lane, and a car started passing it on the bridge. I hit the brakes, and then my car started hydroplaning, completely out of control.

My car drifted to the left and started turning counter-clockwise. Time seemed to slow down. Not one second did I experience fear or astonishment, just complete peace as I watched the déjà vu moment unfold before me.

My Ford Escort kept sliding to the left and turning ever so gently. Finally, it crossed completely over the oncoming lane and came to a rest facing the opposite direction.

One second after I stopped, the side-by-side semi-truck and car roared past. My car rocked violently left and right repeatedly.

Afterward, I sat for a few more seconds and then started shaking all over. Once I calmed down, I got out of the car to see how in the world I hadn't gotten hit. My car had come to rest exactly six inches off the pavement, perfectly parallel with the road. The rear bumper loomed six inches from the end of the guard rail. On the passenger side my car was just inches from sliding down a steep slope.

How peacefully God had orchestrated the whole ordeal! Literally a few inches in any direction would have resulted in disaster. I immediately thought of God's angels having charge over me as they confidently manipulated my car to the only place of safety on the highway.

If I hadn't lost control of my car, I would have died that night. God is like that, you know; He gets the greatest glory and joy, when He intervenes in our lives and makes the impossible possible. As I made that U-turn and completed my journey home, I thought about Ma's discernment and persistence.

When I got home, I called her and told her everything.

Relief evident, she just kept saying, "Praise the Lord!" She had been praying for my safety ever since I left her house.

The compassionate and persistent intercessory prayer of a woman is something to behold and appreciate. Yes, guys and gals, we have much to be thankful for. God has gifted us with the presence of wise, discerning women — whether wives, mothers, mothers-in-law, grandmas, sisters, aunts, or just dear friends. We need to cherish them as a gift to us and our children and also thank them for using their God-given gifts of discernment, wisdom, and intercession. And on a side note, the angels of God

*My Emmaus*

like to have a good time when women pray! May that be the déjà vu of our reality.

*Chapter Thirteen*

## *A Mama With "Angry Birds" in Her Head*

*"For we do not wrestle against flesh and blood, but against the rulers, against the authorities, against the cosmic powers over this present darkness, against the spiritual forces of evil in the heavenly places."* **Ephesians 6:12**

Sitting at my desk one morning, I got to thinking about how much I really loved my job as assistant principal at Irwin County High School. For sure, as an assistant you can't make everyone happy, but overall I thought most folk pretty much liked and appreciated me. Yes, life was truly good.

During that moment of reflection, one of our senior students came to the office for doing inappropriate things in the classroom. He 'swore to God' that he didn't do it. This big, strong kid suddenly broke down and wept all over my desk.

Despite the evidence, his convincing dramatics and steady tears had me reconsidering punishment. Nevertheless, the time had to meet the crime, so off to in-school suspension he went. As I lay in bed that night, my stomach churned because part of me believed I had sentenced an innocent man to five days of

## My Emmaus

purgatory. Several weeks later, I obtained further proof of his guilt beyond any doubt.

The day after his sentencing, though, my secretary told me, "Junior's mama called and said she is on the way to get a piece of the assistant principal." She paused. "We may need to call law enforcement."

I told her it would probably be all right.

Boy, was I wrong! Junior wasn't the only dramatist in the family. In less than five minutes, hot under the collar Mama marched her irate self right by the front office help, burst through my door, and then slammed it so hard that the popcorn ceiling crackled and fell like winters snow.

Inwardly stunned, I managed to keep my seat and my nerve. I can't even begin to give you the content of her speech. That would give this book a rating that would prevent it from reaching many in its intended audience.

I got in a couple of times, "I understand," but not much more. She went on for about three minutes without hardly taking a breath.

I nearly flipped when a piece of spit landed on my lip, but when she rolled her eyes and looked upward, I wiped it off. Finally, she stopped shouting and glared at me in anger. Clearly she had "Angry Birds" in her head.

*God is Faithful 24/7*

When I started to speak, she broke in. "That's all right, you ain't going to live long, I've got some boys that are going to take care of you."

In an instant, I felt like one of those emboldened prophets of old. I leaned forward with great confidence. "Ma'am, it is time for you to be aware of some things. One, Jesus Christ Himself put me in my position as assistant principal, and He has anointed me to do this job. Second, I am surrounded by a host of unseen angels commissioned to protect me, so it doesn't matter who you send to take me out. Nothing is going to happen to me without God's permission, and I am very confident that he will fight for me. Ma'am, it isn't me who needs to be worried."

She never said another word, just turned her tight-lipped self around and hastily left my office. I never saw her again.

After she left, I said out loud to myself, "Where did that come from?" I actually confronted a convincing death threat with the "Sword of the Spirit," the "Word of God."

I had faced a physically and verbally imposing woman, but my spirit rose up. It recognized that I wrestled not against her, but rather the dark side of the unseen spirit world. Ephesians 6:12 defines that invisible enemy: "For we do not wrestle against flesh and blood, but against the rulers, against the authorities, against the cosmic powers over this present darkness, against the spiritual forces of evil in the heavenly places."

*My Emmaus*

The Holy Spirit promised us in Paul's writings to the Ephesians that the "Sword of the Spirit," which is the "Word of God," will overcome the evil one. Jesus Himself is our great role model, and he used the "Word of God" to triumph over the Devil in the wilderness.

Nine months passed after that encounter with Angry-Bird Mom, and then one day I saw Junior walking down the hall toward me. As a high school graduate fresh out of Army boot camp, he looked sharp in his perfectly fitted uniform. He stopped steps from me and saluted. "Mr. Parker, last year I made a fool of myself, and I just wanted to tell you I am sorry for disrespecting you. I ask that you forgive me for my behavior."

My smile made clear my appreciation. "Son, no problem, all is forgiven. I'm just so thankful that you have my family's back."

"Yes, Sir." He saluted again.

I did more than salute him back; I gave him a confirming handshake and a grateful hug. Then I prayed with him that God would protect him throughout his time of service.

As he walked off, I wondered if Mama had also changed. I may never know this side of heaven, but one thing I did know — Junior would indeed be a difference maker.

*Chapter Fourteen*

# *She Likes Me She Likes Me Not*

*"For am I now seeking the approval of man, or of God? Or am I trying to please man? If I were still trying to please man, I would not be a servant of Christ."* **Galatians 1:10**

It is human nature to desire the approval of other people…to be liked. This unseen badge of recognition is so desirable that it dominates our modern social media experience.

Many individuals are basing their self-worth on the number of likes or dislikes that they accumulate. And this all or nothing approval, more often than not, usually regards the most insignificant of concerns. The attention it generates can be intoxicating. Generally, this creates an even greater need for the approval of others - both friends, family, and strangers.

What is it that drives such emotionally addictive behavior? In my opinion, based on cultural observations, the rotten egg at the center of this whirlwind of activity is primarily a deep-seated sense of insecurity.

*My Emmaus*

This appetite for approval never says enough. It is like an obese child and a box of chocolates, one piece will never satisfy. In fact the child may voraciously consume the whole box in one setting.

Just like a drug, this craving for sugar will never be satisfied and likely lead to even greater indulgences. So too are the likes provided on social media. "Just one more like is all I need", says the junky.

The worst of it all is when the need for approval is transferred from Instagram, Facebook, and Snapchat to real life. Why? Because the real life interaction between us and those we seek approval from can lead to poor, misguided decisions that may have undesirable consequences.

God warns us in His word not to let the approval of man dominate our lives, but rather that we live life in such a way that we realize His gracious approval. This approval by God will lead to an abundance of favor, from both God and man. Jesus knew this reality. We read in Luke 2:52, "And Jesus increased in wisdom and in stature and in favor with God and man." However, during His ministry, He also knew what it was like to experience the great disfavor of men.

All that being said Jesus ultimately knew His Father's approval was all that mattered. You see, man's approval is fleeting. People will line the streets with palm branches in your honor, and sing Hosanna in the highest one day and later on nail you to a cross.

Are you and I seeking the approval of man or are we seeking the approval of God? With God's approval we can know the faith, hope, love, joy, and peace that we are looking for. Contrarily, seeking the approval of others will only fester the sore of insecurity. Let us turn our insecurities into the real security of experiencing the fruit of a confident relationship with God through Christ.

On my road to Emmaus, and yours, we have all experienced the joy and pain of worldly approval. Sadly, in the long run it is terribly fleeting. It leaves us hurting and abandoned on the road side in need of a good Samaritan. This is actually a lesson that we may have to learn more than once. In such cases may we always respond like the 'Prodigal Son' and fall into the welcoming and loving arms of our Father.

## Chapter Fifteen

## *Shaq Time*

*"And Jesus answered them, "Have faith in God. Truly, I say to you, whoever says to this mountain, 'Be taken up and thrown into the sea,' and does not doubt in his heart, but believes that what he says will come to pass, it will be done for him. Therefore I tell you, whatever you ask in prayer, believe that you have received it, and it will be yours. And whenever you stand praying, forgive, if you have anything against anyone, so that your Father also who is in heaven may forgive you your trespasses."* **Mark 11:22-25**

A friend and I were speaking the other day about who was the most liked celebrity we knew. We came to the conclusion that such an honor would likely be bestowed on Shaquille O'Neal. Strike up the band! Congratulations Shaq! You are the man! Why is Shaq so likable? Well, he works hard at portraying the image of being likeable and a people pleaser. And that isn't a bad thing for all of us to work on to some extent. As long as it is genuine and we don't base our self-worth on the outcomes.

At any rate, I would love to be Shaq's friend, wouldn't you. I mean it could be us riding around with him every day instead of 'The General'. A free pass to Burger King for lunch. Shooting some hoops at mid-day. Putting on some Icy Hot and chugging down some Muscle Milk after beating Shaq in a game of 21, and swinging by Papa Johns to grab a couple of pizzas on the way to hang out at Shaq's place. Somebody wake me up from this dream. Yes, Shaq is one well liked and compensated guy.

But Rome wasn't built in a day and neither was Shaq's empire. He spent two and a half decades in the NBA building name recognition and fan loyalty. Along the way he won four NBA Championships and one Most Valuable Player award. That my friends is a lot of blood, sweat, tears and perseverance.

What are some other interesting facts about Shaq? Well, he was raised by his Baptist mother, Lucille, and his Muslim stepfather, Phillip 'Phil' Harrison. Phil was a career Army sergeant and he assumed the primary fatherly role in Shaq's life.

So how did that family arrangement affect Shaq spiritually? Author Robin Wright and the Los Angeles Times have identified O'Neal as a Muslim. However O'Neal has said, "I'm Muslim, I'm Jewish, I'm Buddhist, I'm everybody because I'm a people person" (Source: Wikipedia).

Yes, Shaq may be the ultimate people person. What incredible natural abilities and personality God has given him. However, to whom much is given, much is required.

I personally believe Shaq is just scratching the surface of his life's potential. Which brings us to the central theme of this chapter. God loves Shaq and has a plan for his life, and that plan

*My Emmaus*

completely revolves around a personal relationship with Him, through Jesus Christ His Son. My prayer is that Shaq reads 'My Emmaus' and prays the pray of salvation located in the back of this book.

Nevertheless, I am exceedingly confident that Shaq is going to give his heart to Jesus and become one of the greatest Ambassadors of Christ that this ole World has ever known. Why am I so confident? Because God has been specifically involved in Shaq's life for a long, long time. I know from personal experience that God drafted me as a member of the get Shaq dream team two and a half decades ago.

For a brief moment hit the pause button on your reading and refill your coffee mug and then rejoin me in reading first-hand about the love God has for Shaq. Okay, your back! Well let's get this story rolling. Jan and I loved our little church in the country, DeBerry Baptist church, and looked forward to attending every service. One service was on the day of the 1992 NBA Lottery pick.

Personally, I was a Boston Celtics fan and not an Orlando Magic fan, so I didn't give the Magic much thought. But God was thinking about them, and that can be truly magical. Yes sir, the stars were lining up for the Magic...God had a plan.

We were about half-way through the praise and worship service and I was completely focused on enjoying the presence of God. Now I didn't hear an audible voice, but it was perfectly clear when the Holy Spirit specifically spoke to me, "Mike go to the altar and pray that Shaquille O'Neal goes to the Orlando Magic." What was that? A passing thought of my own fabrication? No, it clearly was God because I was already squirming in my seat.

"God, I can't go to the altar. People will think that something is troubling me." Something was troubling me, my own stinking pride. See God was going to take care of two things at once. He was going to humble me and as a result send Shaq to the Magic. I squirmed around for about a half a verse and then made my way to the altar (yes, I was the only one at the alter). I could sense everyone's eyes on me, wondering what was troubling me.

Humbled, I prayed that the Magics ping pong ball would be selected, invariably sending Shaquille O'Neal to Orlando. After praying, the Holy Spirit revealed to me that He wanted Shaq to be under the influence of Pat Williams, who was a godly man and the Senior Vice-President of the Magic. So, I prayed again thanking God for sending Shaq to Pat, and for forbidding any of the other ping pong balls from being selected.

I can't tell you what the rest of the service was about. I just kept on thinking about how much I wanted to get home and see the NBA Lottery selection show. There wasn't any doubt in my mind Orlando was winning.

What were the odds? Well, in God's economy it was a take it to the bank guarantee, but in Vegas' eyes the magic had a paltry 1 out of 125 chance of being selected. I'll go with God's odds thank you very much.

*My Emmaus*

Now I know that Pat Williams was probably praying to win the Lottery and so were basketball fans in every major city, and small town in America. Most of those praying were likely doing so for selfish reasons, but I knew I was praying according to the will of God, for He had given me a clear glimpse of His plan.

What does the bible say about praying the will of God? Mark 11:22-25 reads, "And Jesus answered them, "Have faith in God. Truly, I say to you, whoever says to this mountain, 'Be taken up and thrown into the sea,' and does not doubt in his heart, but believes that what he says will come to pass, it will be done for him. Therefore I tell you, whatever you ask in prayer, believe that you have received it, and it will be yours. And whenever you stand praying, forgive, if you have anything against anyone, so that your Father also who is in heaven may forgive you your trespasses."

In the short version then what is it that God wants us to do? He wants us to ask in faith, believe that we have what we ask for, and then stay up to date on our forgiveness of others. That day I met these criteria and specifically heard God. May every day be such a day! Needless to say I couldn't wait to get home. I had never watched the NBA Lottery selection show before. This one would be historic and I was getting to be a vital part of it.

Thank you God for giving me the opportunity of being on Shaq's team of intercessors. God could have manipulated the ping pong balls for the Magic without my prayer cover, but He

*God is Faithful 24/7*

chooses to bless others through personally involving His children in what He is doing.

Let the ping pong balls dance! And dance they did. The programmers must have intentionally let the balls fly around for a good minute before opening the vacuum tube. Unless you've lived on the back-side of the Sahara Desert for three decades you are likely aware that the Magic's ping pong ball turned up in the tube. What a rush of energy and excitement I felt when what I knew was going to happen happened.

So, after all this time where does that leave us in the 'Shaq saga'? Thanks for asking! In the movie 'The Lion King' the monkey prophet, 'Rafiki', tells 'Simba' "It is time". Time that is to ascend the throne and fulfill his life's calling of being king of the pride lands. Also Esther 4:14 reads, "For if you keep silent at this time, relief and deliverance will rise for the Jews from another place, but you and your father's house will perish. And who knows whether you have not come to the kingdom for such a time as this?" I believe that Rafiki and verse fourteen are appropriate barometers for this particular time in Shaq's life: "It is time" and "For such a time as this."

We have come to the point where each of us need to heed God's call to intercede for Shaq. The enemy knows God has something special planned for Shaq and he wants to keep the blinders over his eyes. I say in Jesus name, this far and no further to the enemy.

*My Emmaus*

Through Pat Williams and many others God has deposited a lot of good seeds in Shaq's life and He has used many others to water those seeds. I believe now it is harvest time. If possible join me every day, or as often as the Holy Spirit leads you to do so, in praying for Shaq's salvation and obedience to following God's plan.

In closing out this chapter, It is a joy for me to say that God is no respecter of persons, and He cares for you just as much as He does Shaq. Likewise, He has a plan for you that will cause you to get every ounce of life out of life. Say yes to Him will you? And then prepare for one amazing journey. Okay Shaq, it is time for a new general as a riding partner. Say hello to General Jesus!

*Chapter Sixteen*

## *Red-Headed Bama Fan*
*"Train up a child in the way he should go;
even when he is old he will not depart from it!"* **Proverbs 22:6**

The day had kept me busy — six different courses to teach, each with lesson preparations. In addition to those responsibilities, I would be meeting some of my FFA members that evening for an all-nighter of smoking Boston pork butts for a fundraiser. Before that, I had about ninety minutes of down time. I should have taken a nap, but the tranquility of the backside of our rental property beckoned my spirit.

This cluster of pristine evergreens accentuated with rugged rock cliffs echoed with the babble of flowing water, especially during the active runoff from a midday thunderstorm like on that afternoon. The closest I could get to the Garden of Eden in Coffee County greatly rewarded the five-minute walk. As usual, I sat on a rugged outcropping of limestone to take it all in.

After a few minutes, the quick movements of a thumbtack-sized jumping spider on the rock next to me caught my attention. I watched with amusement as the alert and ready spider kept to the

*My Emmaus*

high ground in search of his next prey. Within seconds, I realized the source of the spider's excitement. A bull ant traversed the curvy crevice below, completely unaware of the danger lurking above.

With cat-like reflexes, the spider pounced on the ant and injected his paralyzing toxin. Just as suddenly, the spider leaped back to the rock ledge above. In seconds, the ant staggered from side to side.

After a couple of minutes, the ant slowed to a staggering advance, much like a drunken sailor making his way up a gangplank after a night of carousing. I saw this as a picture of Satan ambushing a believer and imposing spiritual paralysis. Intrigued, I really hoped to see how this whole scenario would play out.

After about ten minutes, the ant started regaining his balance, poised to survive the whole ordeal. Meanwhile, the jumping spider continued to watch the ant while strategically traversing the rugged ledge above. Just when I thought the ant would escape, the spider pounced. Again, he injected the ant and restarted the crippling vigil.

Over the course of thirty minutes, I watched the scenario repeat three times. I knew I had to leave, but how could I pull myself away from the drama unfolding on the rocks? My heart was silently praying, "Lord, explain this visual, unspoken parable that is unfolding before me–will the ant make it?"

Suddenly I had a revelation, as if God said, "It depends on the ant. Look at this event through My eyes. The ant is a picture of a believer, and I watch him/her just as you watch the ant. I know that you want to squash the spider and deliver the ant, and likewise I to want to deliver My children. They need only to call on My name with enduring faith. After that, they just need to stand firm and trust in My mighty deliverance, no matter how many times the enemy pounces."

In this living parable, we have a perfect picture of Ephesians 6:13, "Therefore take up the whole armor of God that you may be able to withstand in the evil day, and having done all, to stand firm."

Reluctantly, I stood and made my way back to the house. During my walk, I contemplated the importance of God's message, knowing I would reflect on it many times. Since that day, such thoughts have repeatedly brought me needed encouragement and the realization of abiding faith.

Initially, I wanted to use this story in this book, but I didn't really have the right life application to go along with it until two weeks ago. Today the Lord confirmed to me that I could deliver. As I write this chapter, the rest of *My Emmaus* has already left the editor and landed at the formatter. Instead of starting a potential second book, it is now the final chapter of this one. The life application? Well, prop your feet up and let's take a mental trip to the beach!

*My Emmaus*

Jan and I had been looking forward to a week on Anna Maria Island for months. We were especially excited because both of our sons, Jake and Ben, would be able to join us. This island's beaches outshine the rest of Florida's Gulf Coast. Miles of white sand and glimmering water serve as a restorative venue for body and soul.

That first morning, we all loaded up like a bunch of pack mules and made our way to the water's edge to set up our haven for the day. It seemed like a private beach, clear and saturated with sunlight, and the rhythmic pounding of the surf enhanced a postcard scene with audio. After a few hours of relaxation and tanning, we all headed up for lunch and then returned.

As I enjoyed the scenery, a tall, confident looking young man with flaming red hair came walking by; let's call him "Red." As if modeling for a Harlequin romance cover, Red wore his hair hung in wavy locks to the middle of his back. With a suit of armor, he would have looked like a heroic Scottish or Irish knight.

About ten minutes later, Red came by again from the opposite direction. His pace was steady, and he looked determined. For four straight days, Red walked by at about the same time with the same confident gait that seemed to define him.

That evening as the four of us returned from a day of boating, I spotted Red riding a bike. Instantly, I sensed the Holy Spirit directing me to speak with him the next day. I also discerned that I should let Red know that God had the answer to his question.

The next morning, I helped Jake lug his fishing kayak to the beach. I launched him out to sea, and then a wave submerged my waistline. I felt a vibration and remembered my iPhone in my right pants pocket. That morning was the only time during our beach trip that my phone wasn't in the safety of my shirt pocket.

Aggravated at my inattention, I yanked the phone out. The screen turned white with a black apple in the center. In a couple of seconds, it vibrated again, and then the whole screen went black.

My six-hundred-dollar iPhone had died. My whole morning ruined, I grieved for losses both financial and personal (contacts).

I lay on my beach towel to sleep. But before slumber took hold, I saw my iPhone accident as a scheme of the evil one to get me flustered so I wouldn't be spiritually ready for my assignment when Red came by at his usual time (about three in the afternoon). As the stress left my body, I drifted off to sleep until lunch.

After lunch, we all went back to the beach. I lay down again and almost went to sleep when suddenly I felt inspired to get up. I rose at the exact same time Red came walking by. Astonished, I hesitated before acting on being obedient. He was only ten yards ahead of me, but I had to jog to catch up with his long-legged gait.

As I neared him, I called out, "Excuse me, son! You got a minute?"

Red looked in my direction. "Yes, Sir!"

*My Emmaus*

I approached him. "This may sound strange, but I sense you have a question. And God told me to tell you He has the answer to your question."

Such words, directed at a total stranger, will either intrigue him or send him running. Fortunately, they did the former. He looked at me, inquisitive. "Really?" "Absolutely. What is your question? And by the way, my name is Mike."

"Oh, I am _____ (we'll still call him Red). My question is really life in general. I walked away from my faith four years ago. Now I am 22 and about to graduate from the University of Alabama."

How appropriate! With his flaming red hair he made the perfect Crimson Tide fan.

I spent the next twenty minutes walking and talking with the "Red-Headed Bama Fan" and found him a most interesting young man. I explained to Red that God loved him so much that He sent a personal messenger to invite him to walk back to his childhood faith. God moreover desired a deep, abiding, personal relationship with him.

I then shared a couple of chapters from this book—the Fred story and fasting for children—just to demonstrate to him how personal God wanted to be with him.

Twenty minutes later, Red had shared with me several personal things that I must leave out here. I also learned that

Red's family had owned a place on the island for five generations. This encouraging news allowed for the possibility that we could meet again after this ordained meeting. I urged Red to realize that God had a plan for him far greater than he could imagine. He needed only say yes to Him.

Red told me that his mom was at that moment flying back to Alabama; and twenty minutes before she left, they had an intense conversation about him returning to his faith. I shared the "Déjà vu" story of how my future mother-in-law had prayed for my protection and God honored her intense intercession.

"Red, there is nothing like a praying mama. Yours is thirty thousand feet in the air right now crying out to God, 'Father, send somebody to my son to let him know how much You love him and want to restore him. Please help!' Red, I am your ambassador from God because He is honoring your mother's prayers."

"Wow," Red said, and then we stopped walking.

He turned to me, and I said I would be praying for him. Tall Red's eyes misted over, and he gave me a big hug.

I hugged him hard back. "I love you, Red!"

"I'm going to call my mama tonight and let her know what just happened."

"Please do, Red. Your mama will be greatly encouraged." I gave him the name of my hometown, and he said he would try to keep me posted.

## My Emmaus

Then we said goodbye, and I hoped I would see him again next year.

Red's Mama had spent eighteen years raising him in the way he should go. She hoped he would not depart from it once on his own. He may have taken a detour, but Red's Mama knew by faith that he would return. Though brokenhearted, she continued to reach out to Red, believing that God would intervene and bring him back.

I believe that watching a young adult child walk away from his faith taxes a believing parent beyond most experiences. Red's Mama, if you are reading this, please find encouragement in knowing that you are doing all the right things. Red will be restored to fellowship with his Heavenly Father.

Yes, like the ant, Red and his Mama have undergone a strategic attack by the evil one. One that initially likely left his Mama stunned and spiritually paralyzed before gathering strength for the battle ahead. For her four years of warfare has probably seemed like a lifetime. This much I can say with certainty: God is faithful, and His compassion is stirred all the more when mothers pray. Keep standing firm, Mama; for God's intervention is ongoing. Through ambassadors sent by Christ, the Holy Spirit, and God's holy angels, Red will receive guidance and protection all the way home. Sorry Auburn fans, God really does love Red as much as He loves you.

# Epilogue

May I first say that I honor you for taking the time to walk with me through some of my favorite personal road-to-Emmaus experiences. I pray that throughout this book you sensed the presence of God as He warmed your soul and encouraged your spirit. As He did for Cleo, Bubba, and King David, Christ leads each of us in paths of righteousness for His name's sake. Therefore, wherever those paths may take us, we are not alone.

We may have many twists and turns, and even a detour or two, but His joy in the journey will be our strength and comfort. Many times, we will perceive the direct intervention of a loving Savior. The other times? Well, he is there then too; we just have to walk by faith, knowing that He will never leave us or forsake us.

As you have walked with me through these pages, I have encouraged you to fast and pray, to pray specifically, to watch out for distractions, to intercede for others, and to aggressively confront the powers of darkness. In the Patch story, you learned the importance of surrounding yourself with godly companions.

Perhaps we learned one of life's greatest lessons in "Here Comes Fred," that we should adapt to God's plans instead of adamantly sticking to our own. The Lord definitely wants us to use our gifts for His glory. I learned through 22 years as a public school administrator and a "son of encouragement" that building up others can fulfill that calling. Paul told the Thessalonians to do that very thing–to encourage one another.

*My Emmaus*

If you come to the end of this book and realize that God has convicted you to give your life to Him, then please use the prayer on the next page to call upon the name of the Lord. Then you will be saved. On the page following that prayer of salvation are two other prayers taken from Ephesians 1 and 3. These you can use to intercede for yourself, your family, and others. Fill in the blanks for everyone on your prayer list. You will be praying the Word of God over each of them.

My vision for writing 'My Emmaus' was that it would be an encouragement for believers and serve as a restorative tool for saving the lost. If this book has been a blessing to you please consider taking a picture of the cover and posting it on your social media, along with your strong endorsement. In closing, I hope that your next Emmaus experience will bless you and all those who travel the road with you. Lord willing, may we have other opportunities to share the road together. Remember, "God is Faithful 24/7."

For speaking engagements, book signings and other information, please feel free to contact Mike by email at *mikeparker2018@gmail.com*

# A Prayer for Salvation

*Read the prayer below. If its content is your heart's desire, then simply pray it back to God, and He will save you completely. You have His promise in Romans 10:9-10, 13: "Because, if you confess with your mouth that Jesus is Lord and believe in your heart that God raised him from the dead, you will be saved. For with the heart one believes and is justified, and with the mouth one confesses and is saved. For everyone who calls on the name of the Lord will be saved."*

Dear God, I know that I am a sinner, and there is nothing that I can do to save myself. I believe that as both God and man, your son Jesus Christ lived a sinless life and died on the cross to pay the penalty for all of my sins. I also believe that three days later he rose from the dead and that at this very moment he is sitting at your right hand interceding (praying confidently and perfectly) for me. I am tired of living my life my way and now I want you to live your life through me. I trust you this very moment to save me, and I receive Jesus Christ as the Lord of my life. Thank you for forgiving me of all my sin and giving me a new life in your precious son. I can now face both life and death knowing that you will never leave me or forsake me. I believe this with all of my heart and confess that Jesus Christ is Lord. Thank you for hearing my prayer and saving me completely. In Jesus' name, amen."

## Prayer from Ephesians 1:17-20

Father, I pray that you may give _____ (name(s), me) the Spirit of wisdom and of revelation in the knowledge of yourself, having the eyes of _____(my, his, her, our, their) heart(s) enlightened, that _____(I, we, he, she, they) may know what is the hope to which you have called _____(me, us, him, her, them). To know the riches of Your glorious inheritance in the saints and the immeasurable greatness of Your power toward us who believe, according to the working of Your great might in Christ Jesus. Amen.

## Prayer from Ephesians 3:16-20

Father, I pray that according to the riches of your glory that you would grant _____ (name(s), me) to be strengthened with power through your Holy Spirit in _____(my, his, her, our, their) inner being, so that Christ may dwell in _____ (my, his, her, our, their) heart(s) through faith–that, _____ (I, he, she, we, they), being rooted and grounded in love, may have strength to comprehend with all the saints the breadth and length and height and depth of Christ's love that surpasses knowledge, that _____ (I, he, she, we, they) may be filled with all Your fullness. Now to You who are able to do far more abundantly than all that we ask or think, according to the power at work within us, to You be glory in the church and in Christ Jesus through all generations, forever and ever. Amen.

Made in the USA
Columbia, SC
06 June 2021